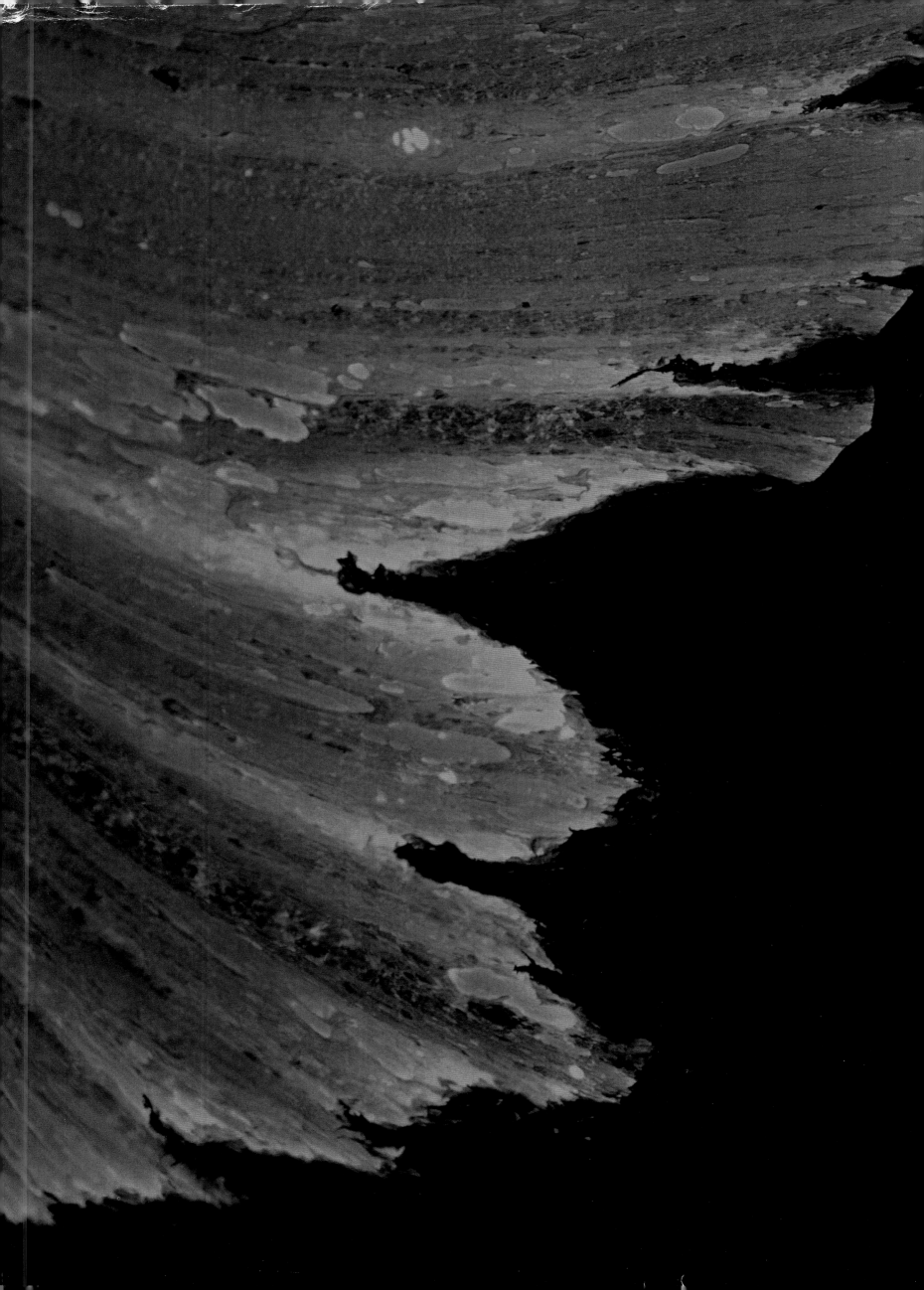

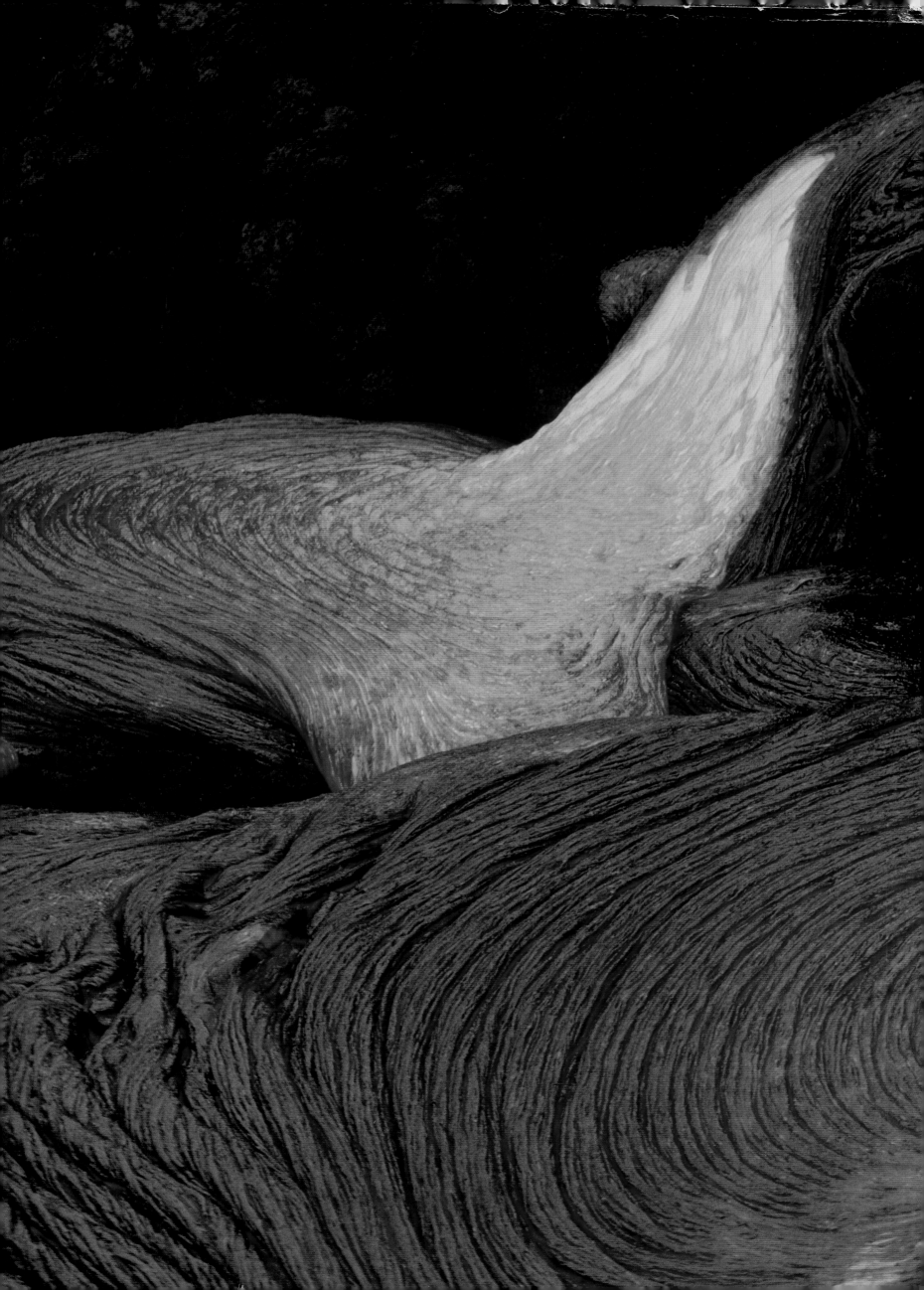

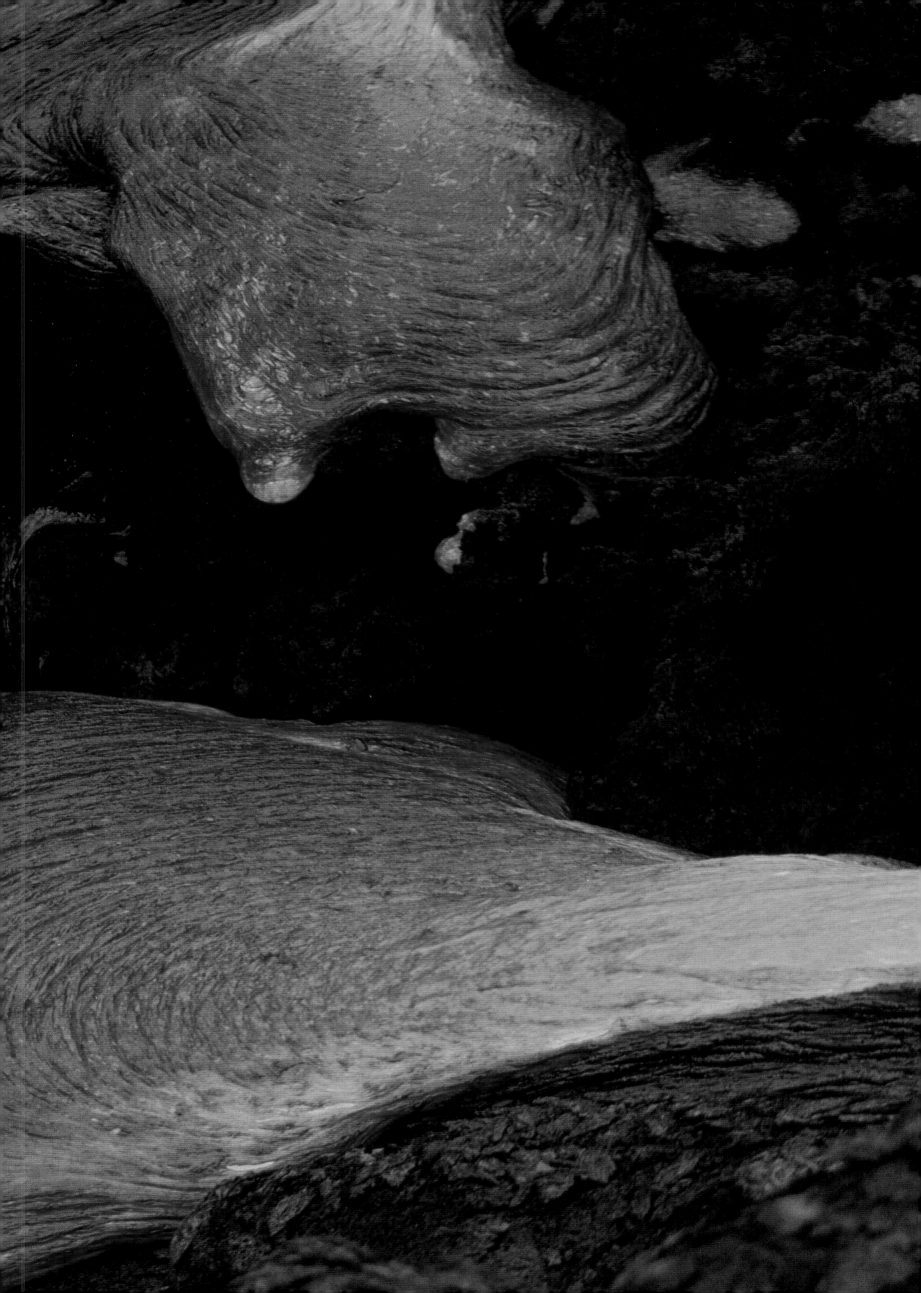

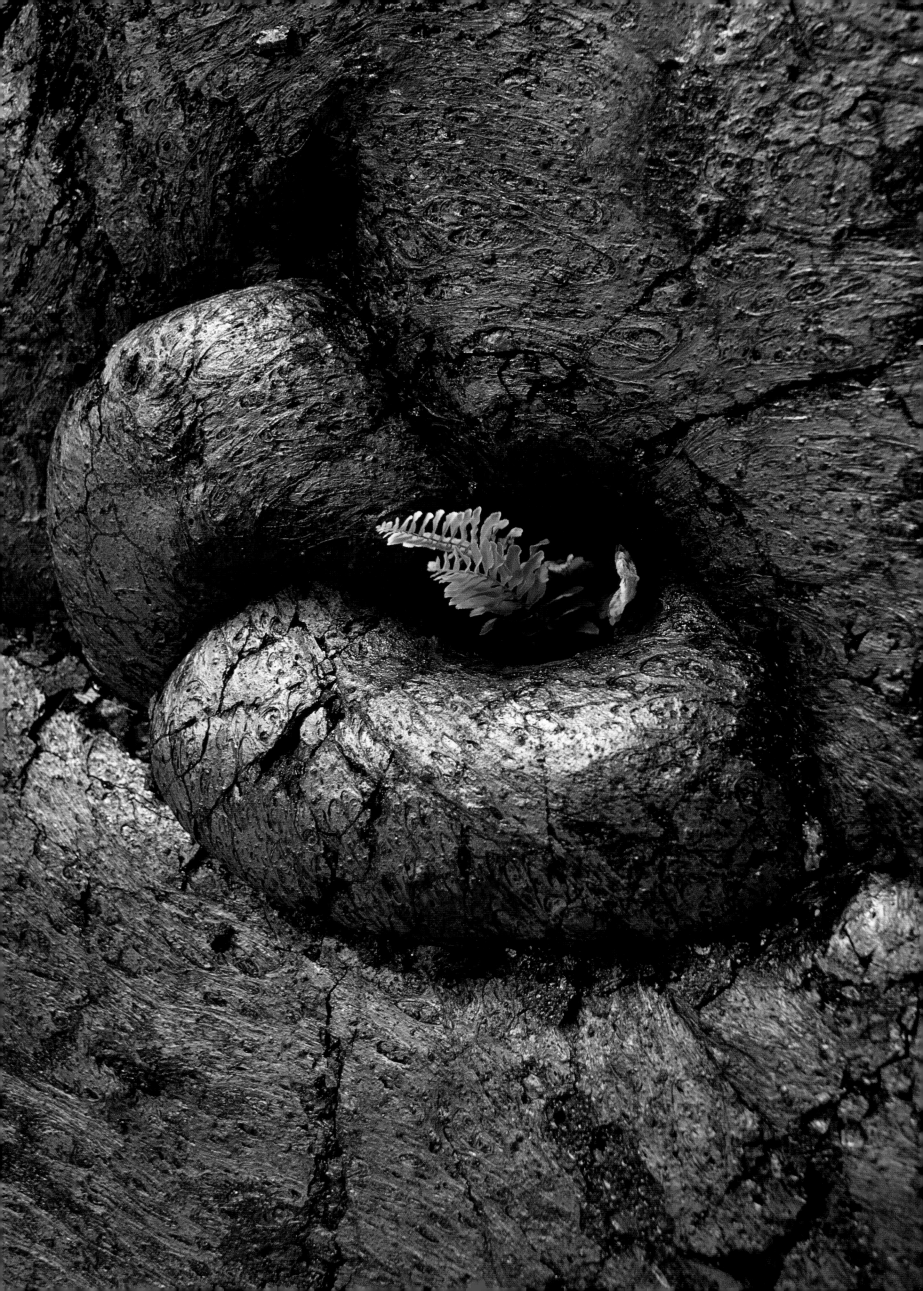

Museums help us reconsider, take stock, see where we've come from. *Discovery: The Hawaiian Odyssey* does this, then goes further. It looks at our history as a series of discoveries: the discovery of these islands by Polynesian wayfinders, the discovery of the body of knowledge we call Hawaiian culture, scientific discoveries about the natural world we share. It explores the events, ideas and traditions that have brought us this far and asks how we can build on this heritage to create a better future for Hawai'i.

For over 100 years the Bishop Museum has sought to deepen our understanding of the natural world and of the peoples of the Pacific. Knowledge of the past benefits us in many tangible ways, as do the values the Hawaiians built into their way of life. This book suggests that in addition to preserving aspects of the past, museums can help empower the present and illuminate the future.

The diverse essays in this book on the theme of discovery are also about its immediate consequence: change. Nature teaches us that change is the very essence of life: air-borne seeds and spores sprout to transform the barren lava; human settlers step ashore and alter the landscape forever; new ideas pull history in unforeseen directions. In our own time, the effects of change have become increasingly widespread and immediate. We can't prevent change, but we can, these essays argue, manage it in ways that will benefit our children and our island home.

Change is never easy, and none of the voices in this book are calm and dispassionate about how it affects us. Some point out that things of value have been lost. Others tell of natural and cultural resources that are being preserved and used in creative ways. Yet others describe modern explorers moving toward destinations still beyond the horizon. What all the voices have in common is a deep affection and respect for this land that we call our home.

Few places on earth have such a harmonious mix of peoples and such a variety of ecological niches as Hawai'i. In a way, our islands, with the right navigators, could become a microcosm of how the planet could be: respected old traditions underlying high-energy modernism, limited land managed wisely, great beauty, good-hearted people.

The Polynesian wayfinders who approached these shores following star-tracks across the vast night sea needed to conserve their resources, to get along with one another, to carry with them the accumulated wisdom of the past. And they needed faith, the belief there's something to discover out there, over that far horizon. We do well to remember them.

First published 1993
by Bishop Museum Press
Honolulu, Hawaii

Library of Congress
Cataloging-in-Publication Data
Main entry under title:
Discovery: The Hawaiian Odyssey

ISBN No: 0-930897-78-1

Printed in Hong Kong
by Dai Nippon Printing Co.
(Hong Kong) Ltd.

DISCOVERY
THE HAWAIIAN ODYSSEY

Produced by EastWest Communications • Chris Pearce, Publisher • Eric Herter, Editor

Designed by Media Five Limited • Kunio Hayashi, Design Director • Laura Vinchesi, Designer

BISHOP MUSEUM PRESS

CONTENTS

CHAPTER ONE

THE SIX SENSES OF THE NAVIGATOR

O ut where the night is still, no stars not much wind, my mind is still too. Steering at night by the feel of the waves I concentrate, relaxed and fully attentive at the same time. When fatigue sets in, I lie down and sleep for ten minutes or so. As soon as I start to dream, I wake up—refreshed and clear. I do that ten times a day, getting two to three hours' sleep in bits and pieces. Sometimes, if the weather's good and I know we've got a good steersman, I sleep for an hour.

We probably once had the innate ability to orient ourselves on the earth, but we've lost it. Now learning the navigation skills of the Polynesians means rediscovering our inborn capacities. Look at what animals know—whales, sea turtles, birds and insects—sometimes travelling thousands of miles to tiny islands to breed. If they're not precise they'll die. Of course the navigator uses techniques and bits of information accumulated over years of ocean experience, but he must also relearn the capacity to be fully attuned to his environment, fully concentrated on what's going on around him. He relies on the five physical senses, and a sixth, spiritual, one as well.

Traditional navigators work with what we call the "star compass": points on the horizon marked by the rising and setting of certain stars. We divide the circle of the horizon into thirty-two "houses." The sun rises and sets in certain houses, which change throughout the seasons. At sunrise, the sun's position in a particular house gives you a known bearing. Then you note the direction of the waves, because by the middle of the day the sun will be too high above the horizon to be a useful steering guide.

You look at other things at sunrise as well. One is the weather. How the clouds come up on the horizon, how they move, their color. These tell you a lot about the strength of the wind, whether it's steady or variable in speed and direction. Dawn indicates whether the weather's going to be fair or stormy, gives you a sense of what you'll need to do that day. Do you change the sails? Should you watch out for squalls?

With the backlight of the rising sun, you read the face of the sea. What are the swell patterns, where are they coming from, how fast are the waves moving? You've got to get oriented to waves, because when the sun gets too high, you've got nothing else to steer by—unless the pale daytime moon is doing a midday slide toward the western horizon. Without the moon, the only way you can navigate in the middle of the day is by the direction of the waves.

As the sun goes down, you record in your mind and body how the canoe reacts going through the waves. If you change direction, the canoe will behave differently. You concentrate on the feel of the canoe, because once it's dark and the sky's overcast and the wind's strong, how the canoe rolls and pitches is all you've got to steer by. This is the toughest part of navigation; I'm still learning it. The fewer visual clues you have, the more intensely concentrated you've got to be. See the tips of the moon? The round crown of the moon faces the sun, which is roughly east, so the line through the two tips goes roughly south. It's not that accurate, but if you have a hazy

night when you can only see the moon and not the stars, you would use that. It's more accurate than steering by the feel of the waves. You want to use the most accurate clues you've got at any given moment.

If you're trying for a landfall on an island with tall mountains, you can see it from ninety, a hundred miles away. You might be able to see an atoll from the wooded side, the windward side, at about ten miles. But if you're on the leeward side, which is usually just reef, you may hear the waves breaking before you see the island. Approaching atolls, seabirds become important—especially terns and noddies. You almost always see noddies close by the islands. When the sun starts to go down, they fly straight home to land, and their path tells you where the island is. Other birds fly erratically, but their general path will be towards the island. When the booby birds are fishing, they fly low between the waves and their path wanders. But around atolls they'll be fishing, and then they'll suddenly lift and soar up, gaining altitude so they can see the atoll. Then they head for it, straight as an arrow.

Preparing for a trip, I struggle with the knowledge of the toll it's going to take on me, and my uncertainty about how I'm going to bear up. I can see this same uncertainty in the two new navigators who will be in charge of the *Hōkūle'a*'s next trip. They don't think they can do it. But when they get out there, they'll find they can. They'll find they want to see everything, know everything about the voyage. They're not going to want to sleep. And they're going to find their landfall, because eventually, as long as you don't give in, you find what you're looking for. It's a trial, a test of perseverance.

More, it's about the pride and dignity of your people, about following the wake of your ancestors. You're not about to let them down.

—*Nainoa Thompson*

In the doldrums, the equatorial belt of unpredictable weather between the northeast and the southeast tradewinds, sailing vessels can be trapped by shifting breezes or windlessness for weeks. The air is moist and thick with star-blotting cloud cover, and severe weather can pop up instantly: squalls, thunderstorms and huge cyclones. For navigators from eastern Polynesia, the doldrums marked the door to the unknown north; to venture through them required a combination of skill, bravery and blind faith that made their discovery of Hawai'i one of the greatest feats in the history of exploration.

CHAPTER TWO

PACIFIC WAYFINDERS

From some beach in Southeast Asia, about seven millennia ago, the first canoe pushed off into Oceania. No one knows how that canoe was shaped. The material culture of its makers was biodegradable, carved in wood with stone adzes, woven of pandanus, held together with sennit. Not a trace remains. No canoe blueprints on papyrus have survived. No assembly instructions in cuneiform have come down to us. The canoebuilders, if their present-day successors are any indication, worked not from diagrams, but from memory. At each stage of construction, the canoewright would pause, adze in hand, to recollect formulae passed down from his teacher, who had paused to recollect the formulae of *his* teacher, and so on, back to dim beginnings when the gods entrusted the secrets of canoe-building to man.

Were the first canoes dugouts hewn from single logs, or were their hulls composite? Nobody knows. Were they stabilized by a single outrigger, or by outriggers to either side, or were they double-hulled? No one knows that either. No one knows what the voyagers called themselves, what language they spoke, what gods they served, what color their skins, what dances they danced, how they traced their kinship, decorated their persons, wore their hair. We do know that they were setting off into the last great province of earth uninhabited by man. The Pacific Ocean, a third

Previous page: Setting
out from Southeast
Asia, prehistoric voy-
agers settled the vast
Pacific. Opposite:
Intricate 'aha, or sen-
nit, lashings gave
strength and flexibility
to canoes' critical stress
points, where outrig-
gers, cross beams and
hulls were joined.
Sennit proved its utility
over centuries of
transpacific voyaging
and in Hawai'i's sea-
slammed interisland
channels, among
the roughest crossings
in the world. Inset:
The claw-shaped lateen
sail, woven from
pandanus leaves, pow-
ered the voyaging canoes
of eastern Polynesia.
Following pages: The
voyaging canoe was the
most evolved of all
Polynesian seagoing
craft, a masterpiece of
exacting design and
durability.

of the planetary surface, awaited them. What drove them out into that blue vastness? Whom, or what, were they fleeing, or searching for, perhaps, over that long horizon? We can scarcely even guess. We know only that the Pacific was all theirs. They were Southeast Asians, and they were embarked on the last great demographic adventure of mankind.

Wherever its point of departure, and whoever joined along the way, the colonization of the Pacific was an epic undertaking. The Aeneid and Odyssey are just anecdotes, by comparison. The Oceanic diaspora was an enterprise of a sort we will never know again, unless, as seems less and less likely, our destiny is in the stars. The canoe people, before they were done, had settled hundreds of archipelagos. Oceanic culture had adapted itself to the infertility of low coral atolls, to the rich soils of high volcanic islands, to the phospatic, guano-based soils of upraised limestone islands, to the deserts of Australia, to the mountain-ous cloud forests of New Guinea, to the rain forests of the Solomons. From where, exactly, the migration departed has been subject to centuries of debate. The New Zealand missionary Samuel Marsden believed that the first Polynesians were "sprung from dispersed Jews." J. Macmillan Brown argued that they were Caucasians; Abraham Fornander that they were pre-Vedic Indians; Thor Heyerdahl that they were Incas voyaging in balsa rafts from the coast of Peru. My own theory is ecumenical. If one can imagine an ancient voyage of exploration, then that voyage probably took place. I believe, for example, that the Egyptians, Phoenicians, Vikings, Irish monks, Basques, various lost tribes of Israel, and all the other putative discoverers of America probably *did* discover America. Human history is long, human wanderlust strong. Restlessness and courage are chronic in the human condition.

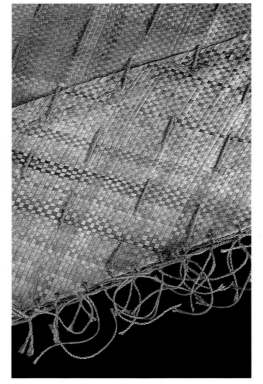

Homo sapiens, the thinking ape, we call ourselves, and *Homo faber,* man the builder. Good epithets, both, but as much as anything we are *Homo errans,* the errant ape, man the wanderer.

Southeast Asian seafarers reached Japan through Okinawa, and ancient Japanese may have drifted south into Oceania—bringing their fishhooks with them. There is good reason to believe that a Chinese junk or two was shipwrecked in the Marianas Islands of Micronesia. Most of the food plants of Oceanic agri-culture, along with the livestock—pig, dog, and jun-gle fowl—were carried in canoes from origins in Southeast Asia, but one plant at least, the sweet potato, originated in America. In Quechua, the language of the Incas, the sweet potato is called *kumara,* and here and there in Oceania it is *kumara* still. If the Incas contributed the tuber and the word, perhaps they added an idea or two, and some genes.

Oceanic peoples themselves are much divided about their origins. For many Polynesians, the home-land was a distant place called Hawaiki, or Kahiki, or Pelotu, or Burutu. (These are just names, unfortu-nately; the myths leave the locations vague.) Other Polynesians saw no reason to look elsewhere. For the Samoans, origin theory was simple and obvious: mankind originated in Samoa. The people of the Marquesas begged to differ: their own archipelago, the Marquesas, was the "Land of Men." The natives of Easter Island put in a vote for their place. Easter Island is the remotest outpost in the Pacific, the deadest of dead ends in the Oceanic diaspora, a backwater of backwaters, a sort of low-latitude *ultima Thule,* yet its inhabitants saw themselves at the center, and called Easter Island "the World's Navel."

Clearly there were coun-tercurrents in the migration, and tributary streams that joined along the way, but evidence

mounts that the river—its source and headwaters—rose on the shores of the South China Sea. In the past thirty years, archaeologists, linguists, and biologists have arrived at something like consensus, and today the most widely accepted story of the Oceanic diaspora goes like this:

More than 50,000 years ago, the ancestors of the Australian Aborigines, in what were likely the first ocean crossings in human history, reached what was then the continent of Australia-New Guinea. (An ice age was underway, distantly, at the planet's poles, and seas were lower.) The Ice Age ended, melting ice raised sea levels, and Australia and New Guinea separated. The Australians, with a whole new continent under their feet, were content, and ceased to be noteworthy seafarers. Their cousins in New Guinea had only a very large island under their own feet. The sea still beckoned, and these people, the early Melanesians, paddled on to New Britain, later working their way eastward down the Solomon Island chain.

For some tens of thousands of years, maritime ingenuity and passion for the open ocean languished. Then, with the introduction of the sail to Southeast Asia, or its invention there—and with the invention of the stabilizing outrigger too, perhaps—humans launched themselves again into the Pacific. By 1500 B.C., Austronesian-speaking people had reached the Marianas Islands, a thousand miles east of the Philippines. These people, the Chamorros, were an advance guard: the first Micronesians and the first long-voyagers. By 1300 B.C., another group of Austronesians had reached Fiji with their Lapita pottery. In a fresh wave of discovery, the Lapita pottery makers sailed further east into the Pacific, settling Tonga and Samoa by 1100 B.C.

It was in Tonga and Samoa—western Polynesia—that the civilization we call

"Polynesian" formed itself. In Tonga, the Polynesian language separated. In Samoa, the migrators learned to shape the basalt of the high islands into the prototypic Polynesian adze. Around the time of Christ, after a millennium of human history in western Polynesia, some sort of perturbation shook those islands. Samoa and Tonga launched an epoch of exploration unlike anything the seas had known. In five centuries or so, Polynesian voyagers had colonized the remotest outliers in the great tract of ocean we call Polynesia. The names of the Columbuses and Magellans and Leif Ericsons of this enterprise are unknown to us. Or perhaps they are known, having entered myth and come down that way: Tahiki, in the ship he named "Rainbow." Ru, so certain that a new island existed for him, beyond the horizon, that he laughed at storms and the moans of his crew. Māui, the misshapen and mischievous being who fished up all the islands in the Pacific from under the sea. (Fishing up islands from an empty sea is what the navigator does, after all.)

The voyagers settled Polynesia so quickly, and maintained such good communication between archipelagos, that their single language hardly fragmented. Much of what a New Zealand Maori said was understandable by an Easter Islander, four thousand miles away. Polynesia was as homogenous as Melanesia was heterogenous. Melanesia was a Babylon of hundreds of languages and dialects. The valley between each ridge in highland New Guinea proved a more formidable barrier than the gulfs of ocean between Polynesian islands.

Traversing those Pacific waters the canoe, masterpiece of Oceanic material culture and vehicle of its dispersal, underwent thousands of permutations. On the north coast of Papua New Guinea, the canoe's figurehead took the shape of a crocodile's head, the jaws wide open. In the vicinity of

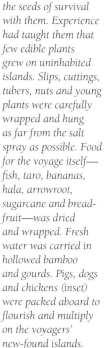

the Admiralty Islands, the crocodile's jaws clamped shut. In the Gulf of Papua, the figurehead was the whole crocodile; in the Squally Islands, it was just the crocodile's tongue. On the western end of New Britain, the figurehead was an osprey, in the Arimoa Islands, a black cockatoo, in the Solomon Islands, the head of a frigate bird, in the central Carolines of Micronesia, the frigatebird's tail.

The sail became square in the Siassi Islands, rectangular in the Hermit Islands, oblong in New Guinea and the Louisiades, pyriform in Moava. Nearly everywhere else it was triangular. In Fiji sails were simple triangles slung apex-downward from the mast. In Tonga and most of western Polynesia, they were triangular again, the forward spar resting in a crutch at the masthead, the mast raked forward. The rig in the Marquesas was the "crab-claw" sail, subtriangular, the base inverted, resembling the shape of a crab's claw gesturing at heaven.

There were the "flying proas" of the Marianas Islands, outrigger canoes which dumbfounded the first Europeans to see them, skating away from the square-rigged ships, leaving them far behind. There were the outrigger canoes of New Guinea's Estuary of the Fly, with prows built up into basketwork shields. There were the outrigger canoes of the Stewart River, bows fashioned into platforms for dugong-harpooners. There were the double canoes of the Society Islands, their paired hulls spanned by fighting platforms crowded with warriors. There were the behemoth war canoes of Fiji, great double-hulled vessels called *ndrua*, their platforms fortified with bamboo ramparts and manned by 200 warriors. There were the triple and quadruple canoes of Port Moresby, the multiple hulls carrying great loads of cargo.

If canoe design was endlessly variable in Oceania, the word "canoe" was not. It was *va'a* in Samoa, *va'a* in Tahiti and *va'a* or *vaka* in the Marquesas. Later, in Hawai'i, it became *wa'a*. It was *vaka* on Tonga and *vaka* on Nuguria of Melanesia. It was *vaka* on Danger Island, *vaka* in Tokelau, *vaka* in the Ellice Islands, *vaka* in the Solomons, *waka* in Manihiki, *waga* at Uatom. The terms for the canoe's parts—mast, sail, outrigger float, and outrigger boom—are among the oldest in the Austronesian languages. They make a kind of *lingua franca* in Oceania—a *lingua vaka*, rather. The shape of the bailer was another constant. The Oceanic bailer seems to have achieved a kind of inevitability; a near perfection. No one could think up a way to improve upon it, and it changed hardly at all from group to group. The *colors* of canoes varied surprisingly little, as well. It is odd, given all their experimentation with design, but in their color schemes the canoebuilders were conservative. In archipelago after archipelago, canoes were painted red and black.

If anything delayed an understanding of the origins and dispersal of Oceanic culture, it was Europe's persistent underestimation of Oceanic seamanship. The misunderstanding began with first contact. Pedro Fernandez de Quirios, the Portuguese navigator who discovered the Marquesas, declared that Polynesian voyaging to the east, against the predominant winds, was impossible. It would have "required instruments of navigation and vessels of burthen, two things of which these people are destitute." The truth was that those very Marquesas, in fact, had been the staging area for the greatest voyages of exploration the world had known until Magellan. De Quirios had met the Oceanic compass and astrolabe without recognizing it. In Oceania the instrument of navigation was the navigator himself.

The Pacific navigator steered by hundreds of star courses memorized over a long

In small outrigger canoes little changed from Sir Francis Drake's description of them, Micronesian sailors still sail the 500 miles of open sea from their home on Satawal in the Caroline group to Saipan in the Marianas. Their traditional pathfinding skills helped confirm ancient legends of interisland travel and settlement, and put to rest the notion that the far-flung footholds of Polynesia were populated by accident or by drift. Inset: Similarities among old bone and shell fishhooks gathered throughout the central Pacific offer clues to the story of Polynesian cultural dispersal. Differences tell of technological adaptations to local environments—and of the fish species that were prey.

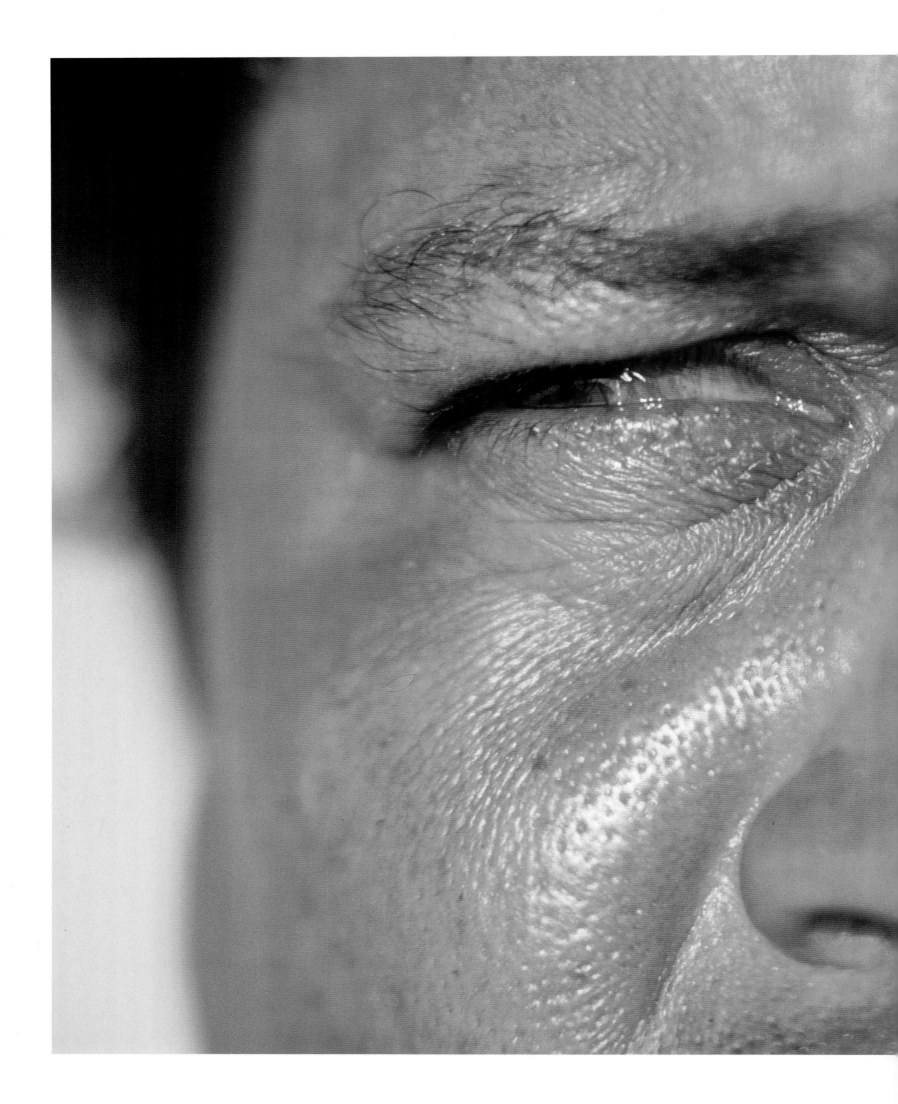

▶◀ ✦✦✦✦ ▶ ◀✦✦✦✦

When first seen at a distance by European sailors, the bold tattoos of Marquesan warriors were mistaken for tight-fitting clothing. Tattoo motifs of island groups such as the Marquesas, Samoa, Hawai'i and New Zealand are distinct, yet share basic design principles that, according to some scholars, suggest a single origin with the Lapita pottery culture of island Papua New Guinea (circa 1300 B.C.), where pottery fragments exhibit similar geometric patterns. "Tattoo" derives from the Tahitian word tatau, meaning to mark.

teen degrees north latitude, and still no island revealed itself. Was it drought in the Marquesas, or overpopulation there, or war that had sent the canoes north? Were they following the example of migrating birds, or simply the Polynesian seafarer's blind faith—so often rewarded—that there were always more islands beyond the horizon? We will never know.

On board, stowed in the hollows of the hulls and on the platform between them, were pigs, dogs, tubers, and seedling coconut palms. In the heads of the voyagers was all the intangible baggage of the Polynesian civilization: the polysyllables of the language, the long genealogies, the tales of the trickster Māui, the taboos, the tattoos, the concept of *mana*. The navigator had begun to wonder about his own mana, surely. He had defeated all the monsters of the open ocean—Long Wave, Short Wave, Black Night, and the rest—yet he could not defeat the emptiness. No land appeared ahead. The bright black of the canoe's paint, shiny as glass on departure, was dull now after weeks at sea. The eyes of his people were duller too, probably—or brighter in a febrile way. In their glances, the navigator may have detected a change in regard for him. The past few nights the Southern Cross, which marked several southerly points on his celestial compass, had scarcely risen before the horizon reclaimed it again. Soon it would sink for good. The navigator had not just left his world behind; he was sailing out of his *universe*. He was outstripping all his references. He was voyaging beyond the last verses of the mnemonic songs that had guided him.

If the navigator prayed, his answer came, perhaps, in the form of a red-footed booby. One evening at dusk, the booby landed atop the crab-claw sail. In all the fifteen centuries since, red-footed boobies have learned no better. They still

regard vessels as just fancy driftwood, and they continue to pause for a rest in masts or rigging. Every Marquesan eye was fixed on the booby. It preened. It muttered squawky little imprecations to itself. Suddenly it pitched itself from the mast and sheared away northward. The Marquesans leapt to trim their sail and followed.

That night by moonlight, or at dawn the next day, an enormous, island-marking cumulus appeared above the horizon. The blind faith of the Polynesian voyager was to be rewarded one last time. Beyond that cloud were no more islands. If later fleets pushed on in search of more—and likely they did—then those canoes perished in the desert of the North Pacific. Ice formed in the rigging of the crab-claw sails, then in the hearts of navigators. Poi dogs wailed, seedling palms withered, and the double hulls broke up in chill, mountainous seas of some of the worst weather on Earth. Beyond the cloud lay no landfalls until the Arctic. So it was for the Marquesans who would discover New Zealand shortly afterward. (South of New Zealand's waters lie the roaring forties, and no landfall until Antarctica.)

The navigator tacked toward the big cumulus. Above the unforgiving horizon, so empty yesterday, the tallest island in the Pacific began to rise. It rose and it rose, until all fourteen thousand feet stood clear. It was the serendipity to end all serendipities. It was the largest shield volcano on the planet. To find a larger one, the Marquesans would have had to sail on to Mars or Venus. They had discovered the remotest archipelago on Earth. The island stood ahead, with its smooth, gigantic, curve. The navigator, steering for it, brought the epic to a close. The golden age of Polynesian discovery ended, and a new chapter began.

—*Kenneth Brower*

▶◀ ♪♪♪♪ ▶◀ ♪♪♪♪

A striking Samoan siapo, or tapa, exhibits traditional, abstract motifs inspired by plant life. The "cloth" itself is manufactured from soaked strips of mulberry tree bark pounded to a pasty film and dried. The Austronesian settlers of Samoa and Tonga, thought to be the ancestral homeland of all Polynesians, saw a millenium of isolation during which time a distinct Polynesian culture first took shape. Inset: A traditional Tongan feathered mat woven from stripped pandanus leaves.

▶◀✤✤✤✤▶◀✤✤✤✤
Over 2000 years ago, anthropologists believe, migrants from Samoa and Tonga sailed far-ther into the unknown eastern Pacific, to the uninhabited Marquesan and Society islands. Not even the reef-fringed beauty of Bora Bora in the Society Islands (this page) could keep its settlers at home. Harsh necessity forced more migra-tions…or was it simple wanderlust? By the year year A.D. 1000 the entire central and south Pacific, an area as vast as Europe and North America combined, had been claimed by the people of Polynesia.

▶◀ ‡‡‡‡▶ ◀‡‡‡‡

Enigmatic stone faces of Rapanui, or Easter Island, gaze westward in the night sky, toward the path of distant islands (the Marquesan, Tuamotu and Society groups), the Polynesian stepping stones that led to this lonely outpost. Rapanui marks the southeasternmost reach of Polynesian civilization, 2,000 miles from the South American coast. Some researchers believe Polynesians must have reached that continent as well; the widespread Polynesian cultivation of sweet potatoes, or yams, a plant native to South America, is their chief evidence. Following pages: Travelling north from the Marquesas across the Equator, Polynesian wayfinders discovered a new star sitting low on the northern horizon, a star that did not move through the night. They named it Hōkū pa'a, or unmoving star. We know it as Polaris, the North Star.

The glaciated mountains of New Zealand's South Island provide the most unexpected landscapes in all Polynesia. The Polynesian discovery of Aotearoa (New Zealand) and Hawai'i, 4,400 miles distant, was the most prodigious feat of human exploration and settlement the world had yet seen—at a time when Europeans thought the ocean's horizon was the fearful edge of the world. The cold-weather Polynesians of Aotearoa, called Maori, speak a language that is closer to Hawaiian than any other Polynesian dialect, but their ornate, bas-relief wood carvings representing ancestral figures (this page) are unique in Polynesia.

▶◀ ░░░ ▶◀ ░░░

Landfall! At least 1,500 years ago, sailors from the Marquesas first sighted a string of high islands their descendants called Hawai'i. Why had they ventured this far north—2,000 miles—so far beyond the universe they knew? And with what sense of relief and awe did they behold the massive, swelling island of Hawai'i with its liquid fire and snowy peaks? Following pages: For millions of years until the arrival of humans, the islands of Hawai'i were sanctuary for a few hundred plant and animal species lucky enough to find their way across the sea. Miraculously arriving one by one over the millenia, plant, bird, insect and snail species evolved in thousands of curious and unexpected ways. About 95 percent of Hawai'i's native flora and fauna exists nowhere else.

CHAPTER THREE

THE KANAKA MAOLI WORLD

Grandmother and I are out on Kāneʻohe Bay—flat calm water, my paddle dripping a line of rings between strokes. Inland, the clouds rest on high green peaks and mist rises from the wet forests below. Shading her eyes, she stares at the steep cliffs, the slow transformations of the clouds. Suddenly she turns to me. "Your cousin just got sick," she says. "We better go back and see what's going on." Ashore, we hurry home and find him rolling on the floor with cramps.

The shapes of clouds, the cries of birds at night, the sounds of waves on the reef—all have messages for my people. This house, the trees outside, the earth beneath my feet—all are alive and aware. We're talking to them, listening to them. We're in constant communication with all that's around us—people, other living beings, rocks, clouds, the sea, the spirits of our ancestors.

O ke au i kahuli wela ka honua. O ke au i kahuli lole ka lani. The opening lines of *He Kumulipo,* the ancient chant that tells of the origins of our cosmos, literally means "at the time of the hot earth, turning against the changing sky." But the *kaona,* the hidden meaning, is the mating of our sky father Wākea with Papa, our earth mother. Out of that mating came everything in the cosmos. Having the same parents, we're siblings with everything in the cosmos. We're all related.

We *kānaka maoli*, as we Hawaiians call ourselves, are in human form right now, but we've existed in many forms before, and will exist in many more in the future. Time in this human form is short; after death, we join our ancestors, assume spiritual form, and come back to our families as *ʻaumākua*—ancestor spirits, guardian spirits. Sometimes we take the form of a bird, sometimes a fish, or a turtle, a shark, a tree, a rock, a breeze, a cloud, or even a new child born into the family. As *ʻaumākua* we protect the ones we love—warning, guiding, informing.

As parents, we teach our young about the three *piko* (centers). The *piko waena* is the navel, the memory of the link between mother and child in the womb. More, it is our connection with everything in this physical world, this life. It is related to the *nāʻau* (the intestines), our organs of knowledge, wisdom and feeling.

The second piko—the fontanel, the opening between the bones of the child's skull which closes as the child matures—is the *piko poʻo* (head center). Our personal spirit connects through this piko with the spirits of our ancestors—back through time to the beginnings of all genealogies, out into the natural world where they live among us now as *ʻaumākua*, and into the future, where they continue to live in different forms forever. The piko poʻo connects us with the timeless world of the spirits.

The third piko is the *piko maʻi*—*maʻi* is the genitalia, our organs of procreation. This piko connects us with our children and their descendants, into the limitless future. A kanaka maoli child is secure, knowing he or she is firmly attached to this present life, to the ancestors back to the beginning, to the lives of generations yet unborn. The piko convey our underlying knowledge: we're all connected—not only in the present, but in all time.

In *He Kumulipo* the *kalo* (the taro plant) was one of the early children of Papa the earth-mother and Wākea the sky-father. Because the kalo-child was deformed, it was buried in the ground. Up sprouted the first taro plant. The next child was Hāloa, our first human ancestor. But above us kānaka is the taro plant, our superior, our *hiapo* (eldest sibling). The taro is another form (*kinolau*) of Kāne, one of our highest gods. When we eat taro, we're eating the great god Kāne, taking his godly *mana* (power) into ourselves. Incorporating his body into ours, *we* become godly.

Kānaka maoli gods are not distant, fearsome, intimidating powers far from this earth. They're part of all that's around us, our everyday lives, ourselves. *ʻUala* the sweet potato is a form of Lono. *Niu* the coconut is a kinolau of Kū, as is *ʻulu* the breadfruit. *Maiʻa*, the banana, is the kinolau of Kanaloa. These are our great gods, the gods that our ancestors brought with them on the canoes from the distant southern islands. They brought these plants not only because they are our principal foods, but because they are our gods. As Peter Buck said: "Great men became chiefs, great chiefs became gods, and gods took many forms."

We look at how the taro plant grows and propagates itself: clustered around the central plant—the *makua* (parent)—are *ʻohā* (offshoots), and around them, little *keiki* (children). Collectively, all this is called "*ʻohana*." ʻOhana is also our word for "family."

We see ourselves—parents, children, and grandparents—in our hiapo the taro plant and the growth of its ʻohana.

The land is our mother; our word for it—*ʻāina*—literally means "that which feeds." It doesn't belong to us; we belong to it, and are part of it. If any part is harmed or desecrated, we feel the pain ourselves. Separated from our land and water, we are adrift, without meaning.

))))ミ ミ ミ)))) ミ ミ ミ
*Masters of the ocean's
vast and tempera-
mental surface, the
Hawaiians were
also adept in its depths.
The best swimmers
dove to 100 feet.
An early European
visitor wrote of women
with babies in tow,
swimming effortlessly
across reefs and
through raging surf
to greet his ship. In the
leeward areas where
streams and drink-
ing water were scarce,
fishermen swam
or paddled canoes
offshore to submerged
freshwater springs.
Grasping empty gourds,
they dove down to
the cool upwellings and
placed the gourds'
small openings directly
over the jets. After
a few dives, the gourds
were full.*

Before the Westerners, we had no private property, no ownership of land. We had access to any and all of the natural resources except those few areas which were *kapu* (taboo), like certain fishing grounds during certain seasons. Islands were divided into *ahupua'a*—large wedges of land extending inland from the coast. An ahupua'a often had ridges on both sides, one or several valleys where taro, bananas, yams and other food plants were cultivated, forested uplands, a length of shoreline, and the adjoining ocean. The fisherman fished not only for himself, but for everyone in the ahupua'a. The farmer planted taro and the woodsman cut firewood for everyone. Of necessity, good interpersonal relationships were paramount; life revolved around sharing and exchange.

Practically all the inhabitants of an ahupua'a were blood relatives, members of an extended 'ohana unlike the modern nuclear family. Because there was no private ownership and no property to inherit, there was no need for households with one father, one mother, and their children. In the 'ohana, all the men and women in the middle generation were *mākua* (parents) and one mated with whomever one desired. All youngsters were *kamali'i* (children); all elders were *kūpuna* (grandparents). No difference between parents, aunts and uncles; no word for cousin—members of the same generation were all siblings (today's "brah" and "seestah" echo this).

The men performed religious rituals and ate meals in the men's house (*hale mua*), but everyone slept in the big sleeping house (*hale noa*): many generations, many people. Kānaka maoli children learned early about sex and childbirth. In the 'ohana of ordinary farmers and fishermen, permanent couples certainly existed, but this was not the rule and there were no separate dwellings for them.

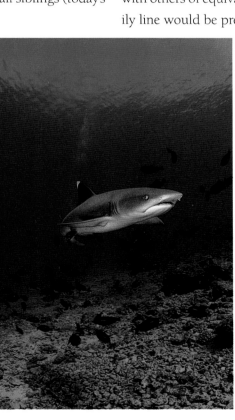

We kānaka maoli see sex everywhere in nature; the link between creation and procreation is direct and obvious to us. Our gods are human. Our *hula ma'i* celebrate the proud genitals and sexual exploits of our chiefs. Often in the morning, I look up towards the Pali pass and see the wind blowing the rain in a shimmering curtain down Nu'uanu Valley, and know that rain is the semen of Wākea the sky-father impregnating Papa, our earth-mother. The opening lines of our beloved Queen Lili'uokalani's famous *Aloha 'Oe* speak of the proud rain on the cliff creeping into the forest, seeking the bud of the lehua—the male seeking the female. There are songs about *maile* wrapped around a flower lei—male entwined with female. Kānaka maoli songs and chants may use different images, but most are celebrating the same thing: the joining of the male with the female. The cosmos was created, and continues to be created, by the mating of Papa and Wākea: "the hot earth turning against the changing heaven." We see sexuality as a central fact of nature: out of mating comes new life.

Among the *ali'i* (the ruling chiefs and their relatives) genealogy was of the utmost importance; certified lineage was the basis of authority. Special chanters were employed to memorize the genealogies of chiefs and high ali'i. The high-born took great care to mate with others of equivalent rank, so the *mana* of a family line would be preserved.

Mana—special spiritual or personal power—comes from two main sources. One is rank at birth: ali'i are born with more mana than commoners; higher-born ali'i, more mana than lesser-born. The other is training: a skilled carver, fisherman, chanter, navigator, physician or dancer, developing increasingly refined abilities, gradually acquires this kind of mana. These skills require long apprenticeship,

)))) ᶻ ᶻ ᶻ)))) ᶻ ᶻ ᶻ
The Hawaiian family was guided by a complex system of god-like family spirits, or 'aumākua. Gods from the Polynesian pantheon—Lono, Kū, Kāne and Kanaloa—are 'aumākua akua. Spirits of a family's honored ancestors are 'aumākua kūpuna. Lastly, creatures or natural objects might be 'aumākua kaku'ai, beings into which a revered ancestor's bones (the receptacles of spirit) have been transformed. The honu, or green sea turtle, is a frequent 'aumakua kaku'ai among the families of fishermen, who came to know the individual turtles inhabiting particular coves or fishing spots. Inset: Manō, or sharks, were also objects of ancestral honor. Many tales recount how shark gods came to the aid of human relatives—or dragged their enemies into the deep.

and one's specialized knowledge shouldn't be too readily shared with others lest its power be diminished. *Hūnā*—certain confidential, secret aspects of the skill—requires the understanding of how numerous forces interact, the maintenance of certain kinds of protocol, and the observance of strict kinds of behavior and attention. Chants and dances have to be done impeccably, as do rituals. There is a *right* way to do everything; even the smallest daily activity exists in a web of belief and practice.

When we chant—in ritual, prayer, or accompanying the hula—if the words and songs are uttered properly, they carry with them the power to do things. We don't merely petition our gods to do something and hope they'll do it; we *participate* in the doing of it by the *way* we ask; the belief, the ritual, and the result all become one. And our prayers are two-way communications between humans and gods; we're prepared to receive responses in whatever form they may come: patterns in the fire, images in a dream, a sudden gust of wind, a grumble of thunder, a thought that seems to come from nowhere. We know nothing comes from nowhere; everything has causes, and exists for a reason.

What troubles us most is an angry misunderstanding, a relationship that's gone out of balance. We try not to confront another kanaka; we'll often pretend a difference doesn't exist, or try to resolve an imbalance by edging up to it obliquely, hoping it will resolve itself. Direct confrontation requires going through a formal process of resolution; if this fails, violence may result.

One way of maintaining balance is by *mo'olelo,* "talking story." It may look like we're just sitting and chatting, but really, we're building trust and emphasizing what we have in common. Our differences in other settings—teacher and student, grandparent and grandchild, hiapo and younger sibling—are ignored as we talk casually, informally, comfortably, without pretense or ceremony Traditionally we'll start talking story with a stranger by asking about personal things: where does he or she come from? Does he or she know so-and-so? And almost invariably—all of us being kānaka maoli—if we talk long enough we'll find out we're *related.*

The question arises: why warfare in a society so dedicated to maintaining harmony and proper relationships? To some degree, one could say wars were fought to restore balance (*pono*). But to some degree, I think the first Westerners may have exaggerated warfare's importance in Hawaiian society, and misunderstood its role. At the time of Captain Cook's arrival in 1778, there *was* great rivalry between Kamehameha and the other high chiefs. Commoners were conscripted into their armies, and historian Samuel Kamakau later wrote of "merciless battles…in which the earth was literally covered with the innocent who were slaughtered." But in earlier times, warfare had important elements of ritual and sport, as groups in the warrior class tested their strength against each other, and it rarely disrupted the lives of the commoners.

The arrival of the Westerners intensified the bloodshed. Western concepts about the acquisition of material goods—control of the sandalwood trade, for example—became war goals. The natural world became "natural resources"— no longer a sacred extension of our 'ohana, alive with the spirits of our ancestors. When Kamehameha started using Western guns and advisors, the level of violence escalated.

This is not to suggest that the traditional kanaka maoli world was without violence. Oral history holds that the high priest (*kahuna*) Pa'ao brought a strict new religion from Tahiti in about the 13th century, greatly

))))ᏃᏃᏃ))))) ᏃᏃᏃ

For Hawaiians, the forest was a forbidding land of ghosts and gods, but it was also a living warehouse. The misty, bird-twittering silence of the woodlands might be broken by the rustle of a kahuna lāʻau lapaʻau, or medical priest, gathering pōpolo leaves; the mutterings of a hahai manu, or birdcatcher, stalking a nest of ʻōʻō birds for their precious yellow feathers; or by an entire army of priests and laborers chipping away at the base of a towering koa tree with their adzes, its trunk destined to slip over ocean swells as a war canoe. Following pages: While the Hawaiian sailing canoe (pages 20-21) was superbly adapted to the demands of interisland and open-ocean voyaging, in coastal waters thousands of smaller fishing canoes brought home the catch to a growing population.

increasing the power of the ali'i, meting out harsh punishments for the breaking of new kapu, and introducing new rituals and ceremonies—including human sacrifice. Rivalry increased between chiefs for political control. For the first time, Hawai'i had an island-wide government and religious system, with *konohiki* (ahupua'a managers) overseeing production and passing a portion back to the ruling chiefs.

But the traditional culture of the *maka'āinana* (commoners—literally "the eyes of the land") continued much as it had for the many centuries before the arrival of Pa'ao. Some ruling chiefs were loved for their fairness and generosity; occasionally one was hated and feared; but in general, we didn't pay much attention to the new hierarchy or the state religious rituals, being absorbed with our work, our 'ohana and our 'aumākua. Warfare intruded into our lives occasionally, it's true. But we could assert ourselves against oppressive demands from above, even to the point of supporting the overthrow of an unfair chief, and we could move to a different ahupua'a if we felt the konohiki in ours was unfair.

At all levels of society, from ali'i to kāhuna to maka'āinana, kānaka maoli believe in balance and protocol. Preparing and consuming a meal has to be done in a certain way. Preparations for the treatment of someone who is ill, such as the gathering of *lā'au lapa'au* (medicinal plants), have to be done at a certain time of day with certain rules, prayers, and thoughts. Each detail in a process is important.

This careful attention to detail and procedure led to a pursuit of excellence stretching beyond what was just necessary to survive, and resulted in creations that were extraordinary by the standards of any society. Kānaka maoli *wa'a* (sailing canoes), their hulls shaped and polished from huge koa logs, were the sleekest and

strongest boats in the Pacific and—until very recently—the swiftest sailing craft on any ocean. Our dazzling feather capes and leis were unique in color, design, and quality. Hawaiian calabashes—gleaming hand-carved hardwood bowls—were prized by the ali'i and exchanged as gifts. *Olonā* fiber was made into the world's strongest plant-derived cordage. Kānaka maoli agriculturalists developed more than three hundred varieties of taro, many of them for dyes and medicines as well as food. Surfboards and surfing were invented here. *Hula* expressed the tales and beliefs of our culture with grace and drama. Walled *loko i'a* (fishponds) extended out from the shores, raising fish which fed directly on algae, producing protein with extraordinary efficiency. Stone-faced terraced and irrigated pond-fields (*lo'i*) filled the valleys, growing freshwater shrimp and fish as well as prodigious amounts of taro and other crops. Vancouver's naturalist, Archibald Menzies, described walking from Waikīkī to Mānoa in the late 1700s:

"We pursued a pleasing path back into the plantations which were level and very extensive, and laid out with great neatness into little fields planted with taro, yams, sweet potatoes and the cloth plant. These in many cases were divided by little banks on which grew sugar cane… and the whole watered in a most ingenious manner by dividing the general stream into little aqueducts leading in various directions so as to supply the most distant fields at pleasure, and the soil seems to repay the labor and industry of these people by the luxuriancy of its productions."

Some refer to traditional kanaka maoli society as a "stone-age culture." This is technically correct; we had no metal. But equally correct would be "plant-age culture"—we were master agriculturalists, botanists, herbalists and craftsmen, fashioning houses, clothing, statuary, and high-speed ocean-going vessels entirely from plant materials.

Yet what is seen is often in the eye of the beholder. One of the first Christian missionaries, Hiram Bingham, recorded his colleagues' arrival among our ancestors:

"The appearance of destitution, degradation, and barbarism among the chattering, almost-naked savages, whose heads and feet and much of their sun-burnt swarthy skin were bare, was appalling. Some of our numbers, with gushing tears, turned away from the spectacle. Others with firmer nerve continued their gaze, but were ready to exclaim: 'Can these be human beings?'"

In the century or so following the arrival of Captain Cook our population declined from as many as 800,000 to about 40,000, due to introduced diseases, and, one might say, broken spirits. Our religion and language were scorned and suppressed by the missionaries. Our sacred mother, the earth, the land of these islands, became real estate owned, bought, and sold by foreigners. In 1893, Queen Lili'uokalani was overthrown by foreign landowners supported by American troops, and our sovereignty as an independent nation—recognized by 23 treaties with other nations and even supported by American President Grover Cleveland—was stolen. Our islands were annexed as a territory of the United States five years later, and in 1959 the population—foreigners now being the overwhelming majority—voted for American statehood.

Today in this land which was ours a hundred years ago, kānaka maoli have the shortest life expectancy of all the ethnic groups. We have the highest mortality rates for heart disease, stroke, cancer and diabetes, the highest infant mortality, the highest rates of suicide, accidents, and substance abuse. One could say we are still dying of broken spirits; that the foreign system that runs our islands is, for us, a hostile environment. Forty percent of the population of O'ahu Prison is kānaka maoli while we make up less than two percent of the graduating class at the University of Hawai'i. We have the highest drop-out rates in the school system, the lowest family median incomes, the highest rates of homelessness. By any measure, we're at the bottom in our homeland.

Our worldview requires being in the natural environment. It's hard—in a sense, impossible—to be kānaka maoli and have our land be part of modern America. The depletion of our fishing grounds and the loss of our lands destroy our traditional sources of livelihood, our way of life, our sense of meaning in the world. I can't see going along with the view that we should be trying to fit in as just another ethnic group in a multicultural society. When immigrants come here from, say, China and Portugal, and their children forget their ancestors' culture, the Chinese and Portuguese cultures still exist back in their homelands. For us, this is our homeland—our only homeland. If our language and culture die here, they're gone. And we vanish as a people.

I have a one-year-old grandson who's growing up in a very non-kanaka maoli world, but I'm determined to participate in his growing up. I want him to be fluent in 'olelo makuahine—our language—and to be proud of his heritage. And to understand the kanaka maoli view that we're all related.

It's projected that in 50 years there will be no pure kānaka maoli left. We refuse to accept that; we've got to do whatever we can to save our people, our traditions, our lands. If we don't, who's going to? What's the point of being kānaka maoli if we can't be ourselves, if we don't have our culture? Feeling in our nā'au what our ancestry means will give us the power to once again be "the eyes of the land" and see the spirits in it.

—*Kekuni Blaisdell*

)))) ƷƷƷ))))) ƷƷƷ

Previous page: Relatives by blood, affection and adoption, the Hawaiian ʻohana, or family, worked hard to provide for themselves, their gods, their aliʻi and their visitors. The haku, the eldest male member of the senior branch of the family, laid down the law: "Nānā ka maka, hana ka lima!" (What the eyes see, let the hands do!) This page: Kōnane game boards chipped into the rock at locations throughout Hawaiʻi tell of free time, pau hana time. Opposite: The world's original surfers used two kinds of papa heʻe nalu (surfboards), the shorter alaia for shorebreak, shown here; and the massive olo, which might be 16 feet, for the great rollers at Hanalei or Waikīkī. A child's board, barely three feet long and made of breadfruit wood, rests at the Bishop Museum in Honolulu.

)))))ᏊᏊᏊ)))))ᏊᏊᏊ

Hawaiian chiefdoms were ever-changing, constantly expanded or lost by warfare and fragmented by internal rebellion. In the mid-18th century there were 24 major battles in the islands, "merciless battles…in which the earth was literally covered with the innocent who were slaughtered," according to historian Samuel Kamakau. The time for battle was fixed by the ali'i nui, the high chief, after word from his kilokilo, or astrologer, after secret consultation with his kālaimoku, or chief of staff, and after conference with his assembled chiefs. The kālaimoku decided the battle strategy and assembled troops from among the ali'i class, from the class of warriors called pū'ali and from the maka-'āinana, or commoners. The usual weapons were shark-tooth knives, wooden spears, clubs and rocks.

)))333))))) 333
*This page: The
great procreative god
Kāne showed himself in
the many rains of
Hawai'i—each of them
named—and in the
rainbow. Opposite:
Thought to be an image
of Kūka'ilimoku,
the famous war god of
Kamehameha I,
this well-preserved
'aumakua hulu manu
is covered with thou-
sands of red 'i'iwi,
yellow 'ō'ō, and black
'ō'ō bird feathers.
Following pages: The
heiau at Pu'u Koholā
on the Big Island
was the last important
stone foundation built
to the Hawaiian gods.
The construction, begun
in 1790 and dedicated
to Kūka'ilimoku, was
part of Chief Kame-
hameha's campaign to
conquer his rivals
and eventually unite all
the Hawaiian islands.
As much as Kameha-
meha paid tribute to his
ancient gods, the chief
also listened to his
two English advisors,
who taught him the
strategies of European
warfare and armed
his warriors with mus-
kets and cannon.*

CHAPTER FOUR

VISIONS
OF PARADISE

One dream seems common to all people: the dream of an idyllic place, of a region of peace and harmony, ease and delight. In some cultures it is the realm of spirit; in others it is real, earthly, but difficult to find. In human settlements with a view toward where the sea meets the sky this vision of a blissful place most often takes the form of an island. What is it the sight of an island awakens in us? Recently I was visiting the Windward coast of Oʻahu and I dragged a kayak over the sand to the water and paddled out toward the horizon. Then I turned and drifted awhile, looking at the island. Above Waimānalo, the sultry, windless air had piled clouds and mist, smoky gray against the dark ramparts of the Koʻolau range. Below those shrouded cliffs, green-black thickets of ironwood lined the shore, and at the edge of this sombre landscape the sunshine broke through to illuminate a dazzling strip of beach. That thin line of bright shore seemed to promise everything, and I wondered if the magic of islands wasn't contained there, in that narrow border between land and sea. Perhaps the sunlit coast of an island pulls from all of us the same deep memory: the moment we were born from a water-life into luminous air, cast from an amniotic sea onto a light-flooded shore.

It may be for this reason that the dream of islands condenses into a compelling yearning for safe harbor, for childlike bliss, and into one simple image: a beautiful beach (add a coconut tree or two for shade). But as any islander knows, beaches are but a small part of islands. I looked at the dark cliffs above Waimānalo, at the brooding, impassible mountains, and it seemed to me that the dream of blissful islands is the fantasy of childhood or the dream-wish of the outsider, of one who visits islands briefly, and perhaps never ventures into the interior.

In Hawaiʻi the dream takes on a particular configuration: *paradise.* It is a term so freely applied here in the Islands that we never seem to question what it means. On the island where I live, the "Big Island" of Hawaiʻi, one can visit Paradise Found Boutique, Paradise Realty, Paradise Plumbing, or twenty-three other businesses whose names begin with the word. There is even a Paradise Avenue, a potholed stretch of asphalt that runs through a subdivision built on startlingly recent lava flow.

What does it mean—this term we use so frequently that it has become banal? Perhaps for those of us who live here, it signifies the things we nearly take for granted, the wonderfully various beauty of the land, the mostly agreeable climate, the spectacular sunsets. But we who inhabit the place are as apt to praise the rugged volcano lands and sheer cliffs as we are the white sand beaches, because this land is home, and we love its faces, *all* of them. In which case perhaps this is not paradise to those of us who work hard to live here. What is paradise then?

The Hawaiian visitor industry seems to know and has offered its view of paradise quite consistently since the turn of the century, in a tangled bouquet of truths, half-truths and total fabrications. (In my favorite Matson ocean liner menu illustration from the Forties, the portrait of a "native" lūʻau, the Hawaiians resemble Italians, the flowers look like Shasta daisies, and

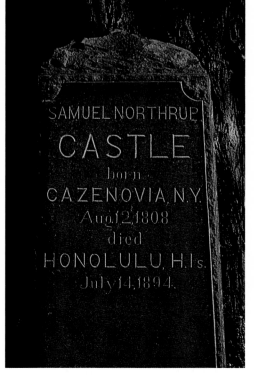

out of an enormous net full of cascading fruit the only one ancient Hawaiians would have recognized is the banana. But why quibble at a portrait so endowed with the "aloha spirit," for everyone is bright eyed and smiling, including the pig fresh from the *imu*…)

Images like the ones on the Matson menu still draw visitors to Hawaiʻi; many of us make our living from the trade they attract. We delight in some of them as our Island version of pop art, and they are mingled into some art forms we love, such as our eclectic modern Hawaiian music. But is it possible that we who have been here a long time, who may even have native blood in our veins, sometimes confuse image with reality? Is this one powerful reason we have been slow to recognize and cherish the fragile uniqueness of our island environment, slow to protect and foster Hawaiʻi, the *real* place? While we offer a generic Polynesian experience to the world, our own native biota is dying off at a rate unprecedented anywhere else. While we offer the ubiquitous aloha greeting, the lei of non-native flowers, the real issues of Hawaiian cultural survival largely go ignored. Have we become lost in the dream kingdom we helped to build?

This is not to say that dreaming itself is at fault; the Polynesian voyagers who discovered these islands no doubt bore with them their vision of an ideal place. Throughout the Pacific one finds the belief in far-off lands, ancient ancestral homes or spirit worlds. Often, the name given is Havaiʻi, or Hava-iki. In numerous legends these places are floating islands, situated below the earth or above, in the clouds, or just beyond the horizon. In some legends these are islands humans may actually find, or travel to, with great fishing, abundance of food, fine fresh springs, where the spurs on fighting cocks grow long and sharp and dogs fatten well. In Polynesian myth, longings

seem to take the shape of more or better than what one already has.

In Western tradition, however, such visions, seem to spring from a profound discontent. Western history gives us a great array of visions of paradise, from sensuous pagan to idealized Christian, from "blessed isles," such as the Hesperides, home of golden apples, to Elysian fields, from the Garden of Eden to the Big Rock Candy Mountain. The extent to which Western culture has viewed life as harsh and difficult can be measured, perhaps, in the depth of longing for a far different world.

What made Westerners attach to Hawai'i this dream of paradise? In 1778 William Ellis, surgeon-artist-naturalist with the Cook expedition, sketched the first European view of what we now call Hawai'i: the cliff and mountain profile, washed by shadows, of the island of Kaua'i. His sketch shows the raw blank face of the land, the skeletal form. So it was not the land itself that evoked the Western dream of paradise, for in the Western tradition paradise was a gentle garden, not the terrain of these rough volcanic islands.

In fact the dream had little to do with physical reality; its topography in the Western mind was shaped by two paradoxical urges—on one hand, a yearning for a lost purity, an Edenic ideal, on the other hand a fantasy of treasures and pleasures for the taking. The two conflicting desires, the one for an ideal harmony, the other for gratification and freedom from constraint, are both part of the Western vision of paradise. That is why pilgrimage and plunder have been linked since way before the Crusades. For this reason Westerners could idealize the Polynesians on the one hand and colonize them on the other. They could praise the Eden-like beneficence of nature in

the tropics while at the same time laying plans to strip the mountains of sandalwood.

Early explorers and settlers in the New World used female imagery to describe the land: a ripe and willing virginity, a maternal fecundity. In Polynesia, the women became totems for the limitless bounty of nature, as the frank enjoyment of sexuality the early explorers encountered fed the myth of isles where all desires and needs were gratified. For this reason the Polynesian woman is a powerful icon (in her exoticized version that is) a walking horn-of-plenty, which explains why the same simplistic but powerful images of her have prevailed in the minds of Westerners.

Around this generic Pacific island female has been built the whole edifice of the modern tourist paradise, from cerulean seas and dazzling beaches to eternally full moons viewed through palm fronds, from fruit dripping from trees to endless garlands of flowers. These fantasy offerings are the campy extremes of Hawaiian tourist kitsch, and we can delight in their silliness and forget that they still deliver the old message: that the land, the women and the fruit of the land form a continuum of the fertile, the welcoming, the endlessly abundant ("Limitless," Columbus said, applying the same fantasy to other islands), eternally giving, forever saying "Yes."

The vision of Hawai'i as inexhaustible cornucopia originated with early Western explorers and travellers and tradesmen but it is a vision we have rather blindly taken to heart. If we are to develop a more realistic sense of place we will need to strip the varnish from some cherished myths about our island world.

Consider for a moment an 1885 painting by Joe Strong of Japanese sugar plantation workers at Spreckelsville, Maui. In the foreground, two Japanese women in the traditional clothing modified for plantation

"Nānā 'ia kō ali'i,
Kō milimili e Hawai'i!
Look to your chiefess
Cherish her well,
O Hawai'i!"

Two short months after King David Kalākaua wrote this chant announcing the regency of his sister and heir apparent, Lili'uokalani, 53, inherited a 97-year-old kingdom coming apart at the seams. The gracious queen and her royalist supporters were no match for Honolulu's increasingly powerful haole (Caucasian) businessmen. A bitter series of constitutional maneuvers had stripped the throne of most of its authority, yet the queen persisted, demanding restoration of her power and restrictions on voting by foreigners. On January 16, 1893, an American warship deployed troops in Honolulu. The next day, the "Committee of Safety," led by publisher Lorrin Thurston, dissolved the monarchy by proclamation. Inset: The throne room at 'Iolani Palace, built by Kalākaua in 1879.

work sit contentedly tending a baby, while a strong, healthy Japanese man stands looking on. In the background, against a magnificent setting of mountains and sea, laborers cut cane while a relaxed *luna* (overseer), mounted on a horse leans back cheerfully against his saddle. This pastoral scene was commissioned by King Kalākaua and sent to the emperor of Japan to assure him that the rumors of poor treatment on Hawai'i's plantations were false. Images such as this and descriptions of Hawai'i as paradise helped to lure immigrants here to work in the cane fields.

Each immigrant group must have had its dreams, a mingling of their own beliefs with the stories told to them about Hawai'i. In the Pure Land teachings of Buddhism, which the Japanese immigrants who came to Hawai'i would have known about, the compassionate deity Amida rules over the Western Paradise, a fabled world of luscious greenery, beautiful birdsong, crystalline waters dropping with sweet music over stones, and soft, flower-scented air. The word that reached the impoverished rural villages from which immigrants were drawn was that Hawai'i possessed some of these attributes, that humans and nature were more kindly there. In China, Hawai'i was known as "Tan Heung Shan," or the "Fragrant Sandalwood Hills." In the Azores, the Portuguese islanders talked of a beautiful island "Terra Nova." The Filipinos who recruited among their people declared that "Kaslo glorya ti Hawai'i": "Hawai'i is like a land of glory."

It was not the "aloha spirit" that motivated the leaders of Hawai'i to recruit immigrants. In 1825, the Hawaiian population was around 140,000, reduced by foreign diseases to less than one fourth of what it had been at the time of Cook's arrival less than fifty years earlier. By 1896 it was down to 39,504. Dying as a race was a very real and ter-rifying possibility, and the Hawaiian willingness to assimilate and intermix with other races during this time has to be seen partly in that light. The specter of a shrinking population was as strong a catalyst as the search for a steady labor force. During Kalākaua's reign (1874–1891), the government spoke of importing "cognate" races to augment the native one. Several groups of Pacific islanders were brought in, a plan to import Asiatic Indians was considered but never came about, and the Japanese were finally persuaded to sign an emigration treaty with promises from Kalākaua's envoy that "Hawaii holds out her loving hand and heart to Japan."

The plantation owners had very different reasons for mixing the races brought in. Plantation work was hard, with very poor living conditions and long hours in the tropic sun overseen by *luna* who sometimes carried snakeskin bullwhips. Most laborers filled their contracts and left—to go home, or to find means of employment in the towns. Some organized protests against conditions on the plantations. The planter strategy was to bring in new immigrants of a different race, to divide and conquer by developing an ethnically diverse, stratified society. But in many ways, plantation society determined the social and economic structure of modern Hawai'i. In their common struggle to better their lives on plantations, workers reached out to each other across racial boundaries. In the years that followed, they sacrificed much of their own cultural heritage in order to become full citizens of their new homeland.

What traditions survived became mixed into the cultural chop suey we all delight in. One of my favorite local scenes is the Hilo Farmer's Market. The market fills two vacant lots on the broad curve of the bay, sandwiched between old buildings and an increasing num-

Previous pages: In 1850, Dr. Gerrit P. Judd, a missionary doctor long associated with the Kamehameha dynasty, bought a large piece of land on Windward O'ahu at Kualoa. Kualoa's spectacular seaside cliffs and valleys, held sacred by the Hawaiians, were put into sugar production then converted to ranching. Today, rancher John Morgan, a Judd descendant, holds on to the priceless real estate by running a low-impact outdoor activities center from ranch headquarters. Opposite: The Loo's of O'ahu gather around family matriarch, Kam Yung Loo (with lei), at the old family homestead in Honouliuli. Now 94, Kam Yung rents out eight houses on the property and travels to Las Vegas two or three times a year. Inset: Kam Yung Loo's mother-in-law, Loo Lum Shee, arrived in Hawai'i in the 1880s from southern China. She married a Chinese/Hawaiian man, tended to her rice paddies and raised 10 children.

ber of remodelled ones. Under the ubiquitous blue tarps (cheap roofing material of choice here in the Islands), blessed by Hilo's liquid sunshine, Japanese, Chinese, Koreans, Okinawans, Filipinos, Portuguese, Vietnamese, Hawaiians and Caucasians, and various human blends, sell an astounding array of fruits, vegetables and flowers. On one table, presided over by a handsome couple—Filipino-Chinese-Hawaiian woman, Portuguese-Caucasian-Hawaiian man—are native ʻōlena (turmeric) and various edible fern shoots and taro, Chinese ginger and parsley, bok choy and wing beans, narrow Japanese eggplant, Chinese, Philippine, Brazilian and native varieties of banana, Indonesian seedless guava, Spanish cherimoya, Mexican sapodilla, local breadfruit and Cuban soursop. The market is a bustling, cheerful scene: tables mobbed with people buying, asking for tips on how to prepare foods they have never tried before; tourists bemusedly trying to decipher pidgin replies. A well-seasoned ethnic stew.

With over 50 percent of marriages interracial, one could justifiably call Hawaiʻi the world's most successful multi-ethnic society. But one might argue that in the 50th State ethnic difference is more tolerated than cultural difference. The pressure to adopt mainstream American norms may be as great here as it is anywhere in the Union. The romantic vision of Hawaiʻi as "melting pot" sidesteps the question of how to preserve a truly vital multi-ethnic heritage. If the only real choice is to live like the rest of the Western world, then in fact "melting pot" is a euphemism for the process of losing one's own cultural inheritance.

I think of the pressure to become thoroughly Western when I go to visit the K's. Now in their eighties, husband and wife, they both came originally from Japan as children of immi-

grants. They have run their nursery carved out of Puna rainforest for nearly 50 years. Their place is lovely, with its beautifully tended rows of camellia and azalea, citrus and maple. Mrs K. shows me a Japanese maple in a large earthen pot; the tree is nearly 50 years old and only six feet tall, but the roots have split the pot, finally, and mingle with the rainforest soil. "The leaves never get as red as they do in Japan," says Mrs.K., "but the tree likes to grow here."

If you buy camellias from Mr. K. you cannot go around ten, because he stops work then for an hour, and washes and dresses in a kimono, and his wife serves him tea. You can go later, but you need to allow plenty of time. If you buy a camellia bush you will examine many plants, for they all have distinctive blooms. You may be introduced to the parent plant of the one you select, the ancestor, its gray trunk as gnarled as the knees of Mr. K. And Mr. K. will detour to pick you some of his tangerines, so dainty you can eat their rind.

Mr. K. tells me that his children will sell the place; the children think you cannot make enough money growing plants. All of this will be gone in a few years, the land perhaps bulldozed for house lots. The trees like the ones in the homeland, that grew deep roots in Hawaiian soil, will be gone. For me a ghostly light filters through Mr. K's garden, when I go to buy camellias, as I buy them one by one, knowing one of them will be the last.

"Melting pot" and "paradise" are related terms; each masks an agenda. I've spoken of the sailor's dream of a sensual idyll or the immigrant's dream of a land of plenty, but it was the Christian view, the missionary vision, which translated easily into a mandate to control Hawaiian destiny. In Christian tradition paradise is the place where humans succumbed to evil, the lush garden

of forbidden fruit. If Hawaiians lived in an abundant Eden then it was Eden after the Fall, a place of spiritual darkness. "Wake, Isles of the South," trumpeted a hymn popular with missionaries called to Hawai'i, "No longer repose in the borders of gloom…"

Many of the missionaries who came to the Islands proved friends to the natives, learning the language and nursing those who fell ill. But they were carriers of an ethic that viewed Hawaiians as ignorant children living in a fallen Eden, a view easily reinterpreted as reason for colonialism. In 1893, when a handful of American businessmen forced the Hawaiian Queen Lili'uokalani to step down and installed their own provisional government, the words "mission" and "manifest destiny" were used interchangeably in stateside news editorials supporting the overthrow of the Hawaiian monarchy. The mission, it seems, was to save the Hawaiians from themselves. As this bit of 1893 doggerel, published in Massachusetts as a "Valentine to Hawai'i" put it:

> You half-drowned chick in a waste of waters,
> Poor motherless, fatherless thing,
> Be one of Columbia's fair daughters,
> And rest beneath her ample wing.

Perhaps it's time for new visions to replace the familiar "melting pot" and "paradise"? Certainly we should not rely so heavily on the ways of the "Mainland," the *malihini* name we've adopted for that large continent to the east of us. Without denying the enormous importance of our ties to North America, we might see what we can learn from places that have more in common with us, in terms of environment and culture. In preserving our fragile native forests, for example, we could take some cues from Costa Rica, a small, mountainous country with few natural resources besides its wondrous rainforest biota, and with one of the best records for environmental protection of any place in the world. And certainly our Pacific neighbors, like the Cook Islanders, have skills to teach us about living in harmony with our fragile island world. But the fundamental resource for our voyage of self-discovery is the indigenous culture of these islands we now call Hawaiian—a culture that is in many ways the articulate soul of this place.

Sometimes, when I have visitors from the Continent, I take them on a *holoholo* I call the "Unadulterated Aloha Tour." We spend a few minutes inside a lava tube, in the pitch dark, listening to a primal silence. Then I lead them across some very clinkery *'a'ā*, the kind that can tear your shoes to shreds, to a remnant of an old stepping stone trail and the depressions and heaped stones that mark an ancient sweet potato garden. I tell them about ancient Hawaiian footwear (usually nothing, but occasionally sandals woven from *ti* leaves).

The next day, if they haven't fled to Kona, I relent and take them to the beach. To Kamoamoa, that is, a black sand beach where there was none four years ago, formed from the gritty debris of lava that flowed into the sea just to the east. At night, if the cockroaches haven't carried you off, you'll see the light dim along the wild, deserted, magnificent coast all the way to Ka Lae (South Point) and the sky to the north light up with the glow from the lava pond at Pu'u 'Ō'ō. The waves pound the coast hard enough to send a tremor through the cindery sand, and the wind carries a hint of sulfur mixed with the lonely, wild taste of thousands of miles of open sea. Every now and then one of my visitors will happily abandon her dream of paradise and stand there transfixed by the power of the land.

—*Pamela Frierson*

Hawai'i's 3,500 Laotians count America as "the Third Country," after Laos, which they fled in 1975, and Thailand, where they spent up to three years in refugee camps. Some of Wai'anae's 45 Laotian families, most of them farmers, send their children to a weekend Laotian language school so they'll hold on to their culture by knowing how to read and write the language as well as speak it. The Laotian Community Center plans similar schools in Kalihi and Pālolo, where most Laotians have settled. Inset: Vuong H. Minh came to Hawai'i in 1981 because a neighbor from Da Nang in Vietnam was already here. He met his wife, Nga Nguyen, also from Da Nang, in Honolulu. In 1991, the couple opened their Kaimukī restaurant, Tan Tien. Their children, Maria, John, Sharon and Vincent, are keiki o ka 'āina; that is, they were born in Hawai'i.

▶ ◀❚❚❚▶ ◀❚❚❚▶ ◀

Previous pages:
The Nā Pali coast of
Kaua'i. This page:
After a century's
worth of advertising
usually involving
Polynesian maidens,
Waikīkī's glamorous
beaches, gentle surf
and wicked mai-tais
are as familiar as
the shape of Diamond
Head, the low-slung
volcanic peak that
is its trademark. With
33,000 hotel rooms,
Waikīkī is one of
the world's most
concentrated resort
districts, the engine
that powers Hawai'i's
economic mainstay:
tourism. The first big
hotel on the beach,
the 750-room Moana,
opened its doors on
March 11, 1901, to a
convention of 100
California Shriners.

Solidad Merino, a housekeeper at Lana'i's luxurious Koele Lodge, arrived on the small island 10 years ago from the Philippines to pick pineapple at what was once the largest pineapple plantation in the world. But overseas competition forced the island's corporate owners to begin phasing out production in 1991 and convert the economic base to tourism. Marketed as "Hawai'i's Private Island," Lana'i has two small luxury resorts and one golf course. About 1.5 percent of the island's total area has been dedicated to resort development; future plans envision more golf links and vacation homes adjacent to the two resorts.

▶ ◀░░░▶ ◀░░░▶ ◀

Opposite: The Tomei family of Kahaluʻu, Oʻahu, has been tending pigs since the 1940s. At that time, 80 percent of Oʻahu's pigs came from Okinawan farmers. Uchinanchu (Okinawans) arrived in Hawaiʻi beginning in 1900 to work the sugar plantations; now there are about 45,000 Americans of Okinawan descent in the Islands, including Hawaiʻi's first lady, Lynne Kobashigawa Waiheʻe. This page: A Filipino pilot with Aloha Airlines, Jay Asentista learned to fly on a Grumman T-Cat and a Cessna 172. Following pages: 300 members of the immediate family showed up outside of Hilo for a birthday party/ ʻohana reunion honoring two of Annie Kanamu Guerrero Irvine's 14 children. In the middle of the throng, Annie (right) catches up with her grand-nephew, artist Masey Chen. The party lasted three days. A few months later, Annie celebrated her 90th birthday with the same huge crowd in Honolulu.

▶ ◀▦▦▶ ◀▦▦▶ ◀

*Previous pages:
Big Beach at Mākena
on Maui: the classic
beach dream that lures
so many to Hawai'i's
shores. This page:
Beginning in 1990, the
State of Hawai'i began
spending more than
two billion dollars to
expand and modernize
Honolulu International
Airport, the nation's
16th busiest. At least
20 million overseas and
interisland passengers,
300,000 tons of cargo
and 38,000 tons of mail
pass through the airport
annually. By the year
2010, according to the
state's statisticians,
the annual number of
visitors should jump
from the current 6.5
million to 11.5 million.*

▶ ◀▦▦▶ ◀▦▦▶ ◀
This page: An early-morning kayaker breaks the glassy surface of the Ala Wai Canal at Waikīkī. Opposite: About 1,500 international athletes compete in the annual Ironman Triathlon World Championships, the top event on the international triathlon circuit, held in October on the Big Island of Hawaiʻi. The course starts with a 2.4-mile swim across Kailua Bay, immediately followed by a 112-mile bicycle race across the lava fields of South Kohala and a 26.2-mile marathon run. Front runners complete the torturous course in just over eight hours.

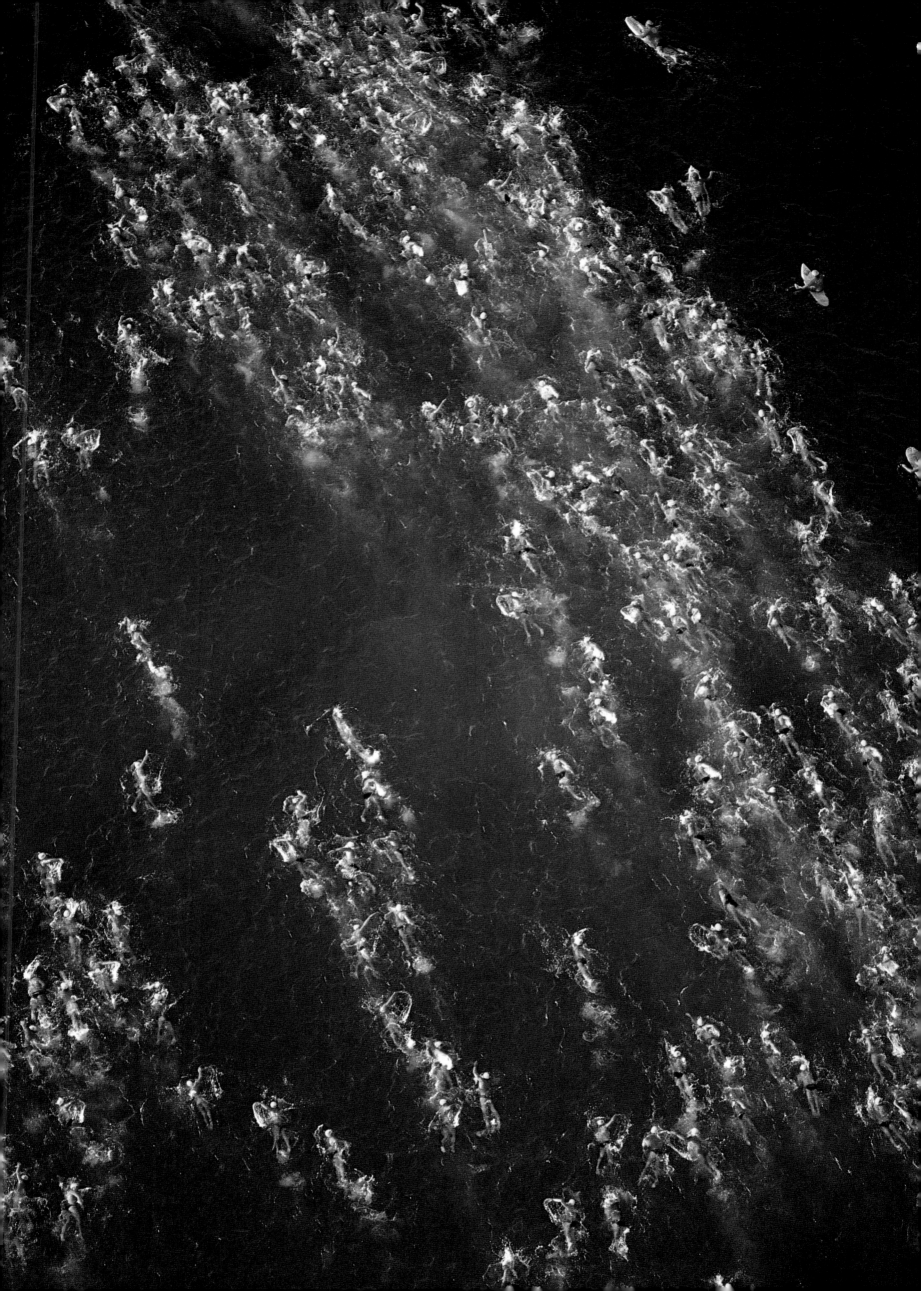

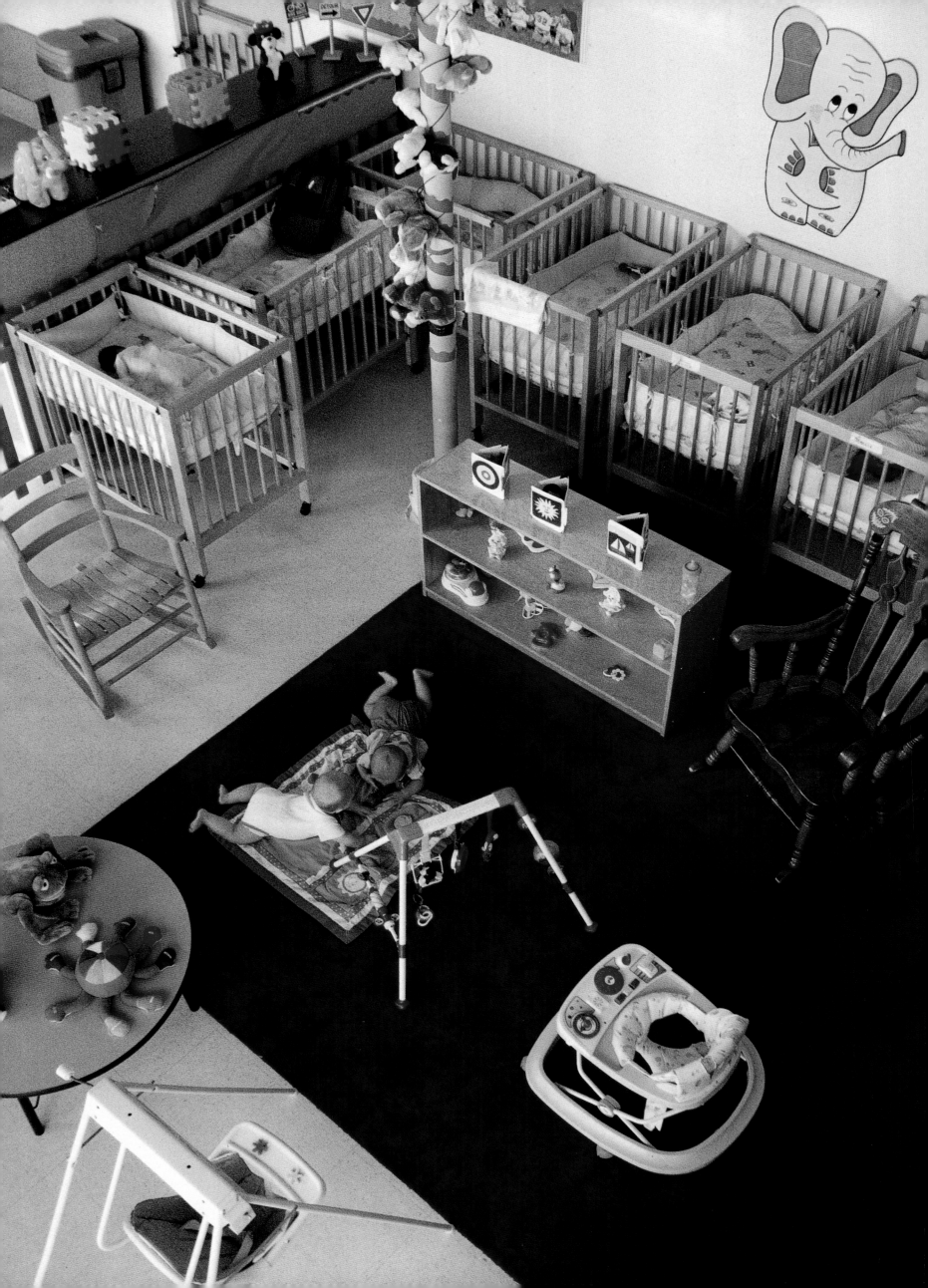

Opposite: "Our goal is to meet parents' needs," says Dana Vela, area manager of the Sunrise Preschool in Pearl City on O'ahu. "What we're trying to do is make it easier to be a working parent here in Hawai'i. The cost of living is so high here, it forces many mothers into the workforce." Sunrise is licensed for 189 children, ages six weeks through five years. Vela says there's a tremendous need for infant care facilities on O'ahu, where only six were operating as of late 1992. Sunrise, a privately owned business, is open from six a.m. to six p.m., five days a week, 12 months a year. This page: Warm water and air welcome kids into nature year-round. Here, at the Hōnaunau tidal pools on the Big Island, Tom, Alex and Nick Choy commune with a sea cucumber.

▶ ◀▦▦▶ ◀▦▦▶ ◀

*Honolulu Harbor's
deep, protected waters
explain the stand of
commercial towers that
now looms above the
waterway. Once little
more than a canoe
passage for the fishing
settlement of Kou,
the safe anchorage was
entered and mapped
by British captain
William Brown in the
schooner Jackal in
1794. Other explor-
ation and trading ships
soon followed, and
Honolulu quickly be-
came the Islands' main
port for the booming
sandalwood trade.
It became the de facto
capital of Hawai'i
in 1804, when Kame-
hameha I picked up
and moved his court
from comfortable
Waikīkī, three miles to
the east, to the very
center of the scrappy
waterfront. The site of
his compound at Pākā-
hā Point lies to the
left of the white-ribbed
Amfac Towers.*

Previous pages: Ernest Kahonaoi and his family live at Mākua beach. When this family portrait was taken in May 1992, there were about 15 campsites on the federally leased land. Opposite: Fueled by foreign investment, the overheated real estate market of the late 1980s transformed several Oʻahu suburbs into enclaves for the super-rich, who built imposing homes completely covering their small lots. To many observers, the opulent architecture of these palatial structures represents a fateful turning away from Hawaiʻi's unique —and traditionally modest—lifestyle. This page: A house in Kapāhulu, Honolulu.

▶ ◀▦▦▦▶ ◀▦▦▦▶ ◀

Between 1970 and 1992, Hawai'i's population, including military families and transients, increased by more than 60 percent, from 770,000 to 1.3 million. The growth, fueled by in-migration from the mainland U.S. and southeast Asia, has affected cities, towns and villages on all islands. Old plantation towns struggle along, beset by termites, rust and a dying sugar industry. Some become resort towns; others wither or fight for survival. Efforts are under way to protect and renovate communities like Pāhoa on the Big Island (right), where Hawai'i's history and its characteristically simple way of life are still in evidence.

Between 1982 and 1991, the annual value of all building permits in Hawai'i more than tripled, from $714 million to $2.4 billion. The construction boom brought thousands of new workers to the Islands, spread new suburbs across former agricultural lands and brought a tide of new resorts to heretofore pristine beaches and coves. At Hāpuna Beach on the island of Hawai'i (this page) a coalition of developers and construction unions narrowly defeated a 1988 ballot initiative that almost stopped a luxury hotel overlooking the island's most popular public beach park. Following pages: The endangered Hawaiian monk seal, the only surviving tropical seal in the world, finds refuge in Hawai'i's protected Leeward Islands. About 1,200 of the sea mammals poke around the isolated atolls and sea stacks, looking for spiny lobster, crabs, octopus and reef fish.

Opposite: The USS Henry M. Jackson, an Ohio Class Trident submarine, carries 24 intercontinental ballistic missiles and a crew of 157 within its hydrodynamic, 560-foot-long launch platform. With eight Trident subs and 35 nuclear-powered attack subs, the Pearl Harbor-based Pacific Submarine Force patrols the largest military command in the world, from the North American coast to the Indian Ocean. This page: Every fall, about 4,000 humpback whales migrate from the North Pacific to spend the winter mating and calving in Hawai'i's shallow offshore waters. Mysteriously, no mention is made of the humpbacks in ancient Hawaiian legends or stories. They were first sighted in Hawaiian waters in the 1840s and were protected by international treaty in 1966.

CHAPTER FIVE

WAYFINDERS TO THE FUTURE

Spring in Honolulu. Luminous clouds hang over the Koʻolau range, clouds with cottony edges and dark undersides heavy with rain that will fall in the high country but not in town. Not today. Seen from the crowded boulevards, the clouds add drama. They move. They send down sheets of mist. They tell you the rinsed blue sky above the beaches and the lowland neighborhoods is a wonderful gift you should never take for granted. Below the clouds high green peaks cut their jagged line. Old photos tell us those peaks haven't changed much in a hundred years. The city has sprawled and sprouted and spread, but the peaks still remind you, even when you're stuck in midtown traffic, that you're never more than a few miles from wilderness, from verdant slopes where no one has ever lived.

It is part of the magic of midtown Honolulu, this startling contrast. In this familiar picture you also see one version of the dilemma facing modern-day Hawaiʻi. As the city continues to climb the ridges and penetrate the valleys, how much longer can such inspirational scenery survive? How much longer can any wildness survive? Such questions are being asked all around the globe these days: how do we balance the inexorable pressures of economic growth and expanding populations with respect for limited natural resources, and with respect for daily life and cultural tradition?

There are no easy answers. There never will be. But something about pressure forces creative solutions closer to the surface. Throughout the islands there are thousands of people, and numerous programs and agencies, public and private, bringing visionary energy to the hard task of charting a future for Hawai'i, opening windows of perception, looking for new modes of dialogue, for ways to join the era of high technology with older forms of ecological wisdom.

Some essential guidance is being provided by the people who have lived here the longest. The cultural renaissance of the past thirty years has revived a rich legacy of arts and crafts—hula, chanting, healing, kapa making, canoe paddling, long distance voyaging. At the festivals you can see new generations of dancers empowered by the reawakening of a dynamic artform that goes back a thousand years or more. With these rediscoveries has come new recognition of Hawaiian cultural values—attitudes toward community, toward other creatures, toward habitat. The word *aloha* has been rescued from the hotel lounges and re-endowed with its full meaning: much more than a casual greeting, it is a way to acknowledge the spiritual kinship that connects person to person, person to place, person to cosmos.

The *kūpuna* (elders) remind us that we are not here to conquer the earth but to find ways to live in harmony with it. They remind us that in the land there are two kinds of power—the power to make money, and the more primal, sacred power to nurture and inspire. If this older power is not honored, they say, we not only harm the land, we harm ourselves.

In Hawaiian tradition, nature, culture, and the spoken word have been closely intertwined. Language has been the bearer of accumulated expe-

rience, a prime means for conveying the Hawaiian way of seeing and being in the world. If Hawaiian culture is to continue into the 21st century, an enormous amount depends upon keeping the spoken language alive.

Keiki Kawai'ae'a is a first grade teacher who believes you do this best by starting with the children. She leads Kula Kaiapuni at Pā'ia School in Maui, one of five schools around the state taking part in a bold experiment called the Hawaiian Language Immersion Program. She studied Hawaiian at the University of Hawai'i, Mānoa, then went on to earn a Master's in curriculum and instruction. She'd been teaching Hawaiian at Kamehameha School for ten years when she moved to Maui. "I had a good job in Honolulu, good conditions, no complaints. I just felt that teaching students in this program was a much more important thing to be doing."

Instead of teaching in English, offering Hawaiian as a foreign language, in her first-grade class Hawaiian is the language. The usual subjects are covered, grade by grade—math, science history, reading—but all day long the medium is spoken Hawaiian. The theory is that you immerse them early, using Hawaiian exclusively for the first five grades, by which time they have the grounding to be securely bilingual.

Critics have voiced fears that emphasizing Hawaiian in the early years will cause English skills to suffer. Numerous studies prove the opposite to be true. Knowing a second language usually sharpens your command of English. Reading and writing of English are introduced in fifth grade, and study after study has shown that linguistic skills, once grasped, transfer quickly from the first language to the second.

Kula Kaiapuni was inspired by similar programs among Maori in New Zealand,

Navajos in the southwest, and native tribes in Canada. The first step locally was Pūnana Leo, an immersion program for preschoolers developed in 1984 by a group of farsighted language teachers, among them Kauanoe Kamanā and Pila (William) Wilson from the University of Hawai'i, Hilo. In 1987 the state's Department of Education initiated immersion programs for kindergarten and first grade at two pilot sites, one on O'ahu and one in Hilo. The long-range plan calls for seven approved sites, with two separate K–12 sites to be erected by 1997.

Pā'ia entered in 1989. It is an old plantation town, now a haven for windsurfers, at the ocean edge of the long plain that spreads north from the base of Haleakalā. Surrounded by cane fields, the school building is a historic landmark. There are 76 youngsters in Kula Kaiapuni, from five grade levels, enrolled on a voluntary basis by parents who often study Hawaiian along with their kids. Kawai'ae'a has three of her own children enrolled, all of whom went through Pūnana Leo.

Inside, Kawai'ae'a's classroom looks like any first-grade, except that Hawaiian words are everywhere, naming the days of the week on the hand-made calendar, filling the long vocabulary list above the blackboard, labeling the chunks of rock and coral on the science table. Each morning the children gather outside the door to recite an *oli,* a unison chant, asking permission to enter. The four teachers are there to answer with a Hawaiian greeting and to personally welcome each child. Once seated, the six-year-olds chant again, speaking to the place where the sun rises, asking for wisdom. "As the sun appears," says Kawai'ae'a, translating, "it becomes our daylight and also a symbol of our enlightenment, and we ask that the knowledge within that light will be received."

In 1778, when Captain Cook arrived, more than half a million people inhabited the islands. Estimates run as high as 800,000—all speaking Hawaiian. By the mid-1980s some two thousand native speakers remained, most in their sixties and seventies. Hawai'i was on its way to becoming the only island group in Polynesia where the spoken language had been wiped out and replaced by the colonizer's tongue. Spoken Hawaiian had nearly died because for decades its use had been downplayed, while English has been promoted as the surest route to economic and social success. This view fails to recognize the cultural and spiritual dimension. Take away a language, and you take away the empowerment of the history it carries, the layers of knowing and feeling embedded in the words as they are spoken, chanted, sung.

Starting with the youngsters, the dedicated teachers in Pūnana Leo and Kula Kaiapuni hope to re-empower a new generation of speakers. "It opens the brain," says Kawai'ae'a feelingly, "to get two languages going instead of one."

For two hundred years, Hawai'i has been a touch-point, a halfway station where travelers meet and ideas converge. In this island world, certain lives seem to be shaped and guided by a trans-Pacific energy. Robert Aitken's has been such a life. As·one of the most respected Western practitioners of Zen Buddhism, he embodies a kind of spiritual wisdom that can arise from this mid-ocean mix of cultures. His book, *Taking the Path of Zen,* is regarded as one of the clearest statements on the subject available in English.

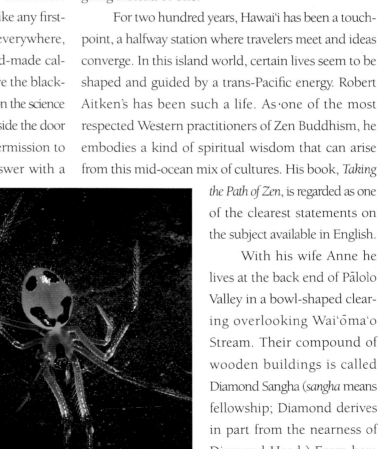

With his wife Anne he lives at the back end of Pālolo Valley in a bowl-shaped clearing overlooking Wai'ōma'o Stream. Their compound of wooden buildings is called Diamond Sangha (*sangha* means fellowship; Diamond derives in part from the nearness of Diamond Head.) From here they reach out to a network of twelve centers scattered from Maui and the Big Island to Australia, New Mexico, Texas and South America.

He is a tall, lean fellow who chooses his words with attentiveness. Though he speaks affectionately of the tropical light, the birdsong, and other island features so many have found to be spiritually nourishing, this did not have much to do with why he chose Hawai'i to practice Zen. "It happens to be where I grew up," he says. "It is my place. The mountains and the valleys are my home."

He arrived in 1922, at the age of five, soon after his father took a job with the Bishop Museum. He was 25 when World War II broke out, working on Guam with a Naval Base construction unit. Captured by the Japanese, he spent three years in a prison camp in Kobe, where he met R.C. Blyth, author of *Zen and English Literature*. "That was the start of my infection," he says with a laugh, speaking of the study and practice that has occupied him for half a century.

After the war, he divided his time between Japan, California, and the University of Hawai'i, where he received degrees in English and in Japanese literature. In 1959 he and Anne established a meditation group in Honolulu, for many years based at the Koko An Zendo in Mānoa Valley. Diamond Sangha is part of the *Sanbo Kyodan* (Order of the Three Treasures), a lay stream of Soto Zen. In 1974, after 26 years of practice, Aitken was authorized to teach as a *roshi*, one of a very few Americans ever to be so designated. In 1985 he received full transmission.

He sees close ties between Zen and Hawaiian tradition. "They can enhance each other. The Hawaiian sense of place, and the role of the 'aumākua in daily life, is very much in keeping with Zen practice. In Zen, animals and plants are not totems or guardian spirits in the 'aumākua sense; nonetheless an inspiration comes from

nature, from the many forms."

The "net of Indra," he notes, is an image of the universe which originated in India, was developed in China, and is expressed in Zen thought and practice. "It is a philosophical model which conveys the idea that all beings reflect each other, and indeed, contain each other." He quotes the 13th century master Dogen: *the 10,000 things confirm the self...*

"It's not the diety," he says, "it's the things. The other beings—earth's lifeforms—confirm the self. Without the beings I have no being."

In Pālolo a new *zendo* is under construction, and a dormitory to house residents and visitors. At 75, when most people have been retired for years, Aitken seems on the threshold of a new beginning. His eyes are bright. His voice is soft. From time to time, like a true roshi, he lets his laughter ring forth. In the end, his very manner is the message: awareness of the interconnectedness of all things, and attentiveness to each word, each moment—all leavened with a heartful laugh which is itself a form of recognition and compassion for the daily struggle of the human spirit.

The "ten thousand things" is another way of talking about the multitude of species that inhabit the seas and fields and mountains. Each year more and more are threatened. Each time a creature disappears—such as the exquisite Kaua'i 'o'o that once flourished and sang in the Alaka'i wilderness—one of

life's miracles is gone forever. As earthly creatures we too are diminished, and endangered, since all living things are interdependent. "Without the beings," says the roshi, "I have no being."

A few miles from the zendo, in a two-story brick building in Honolulu's Chinatown, there is an organization devoted to protecting the earth's rare species by protecting the places they need to survive.

Like a space station, the submersible platform LRT 30A provides an underwater home base for the Pisces V deep-sea diving sub. Here divers disengage the sub from the platform deck for a 6,300-foot exploratory dive to a group of hydrothermal vents east of the Big Island. This unique-in-the-world platform, loosely tethered to the surface ship by 60-foot cables, was designed to deal with Hawai'i's rough waters, where normal surface conditions include 25-knot winds and 12-foot seas. Pisces V has a waiting list of international users including oceanographers, geophysicists, geochemists and marine biologists anxious to get a first-hand glimpse of the Pacific floor.

The Nature Conservancy is an international non-profit group founded in 1951. In Hawai'i the Conservancy has helped to protect nearly 50,000 acres, and now manages ten sites on five islands—sites such as Mo'omomi Dunes, a 920-acre preserve on Moloka'i, nesting ground for the endangered Hawaiian green sea turtle, and Honouliuli, a 3,692-acre preserve in O'ahu's Wai'ānae Range, home to more than 45 rare plant and animal varieties.

Kelvin Taketa presides over the Conservancy's Pacific region. Born and educated in Honolulu, he holds a degree from Hastings College of Law in San Francisco. "I grew up during the transition from Territory to Statehood," he says, "from agriculture to tourism. My grandfather had a ranch on the slopes of Olomana on windward O'ahu, where I spent a great deal of time. That is where I learned to love the outdoors and the land. I learned from my grandfather and others like him how to work with people instead of working against them. That's still the best way to get things done in Hawai'i." This trait has served Taketa well in the Nature Conservancy, which looks for ways to bring people together—public and private, corporate and federal.

In fall 1991 the Conservancy co-authored a landmark report entitled *Hawai'i's Extinction Crisis: A Call to Action*. It stirred a national media response, with coverage on ABC's "Saturday Evening News." For Taketa, who spends long hours in behind-the-scenes diplomacy, the real achievement was to be found on the credits page. It listed three organizations responsible for the report: The Nature Conservancy of Hawai'i, the state's Department of Land and Natural Resources, and the U.S. Fish and Wildlife Service.

"Symbolically this was very important. As far as I know there's never been anything like it before—the state, the fed-

eral government and a private group able to issue a joint statement of this magnitude about the environmental crisis, and actually agree on the language."

The message was strong and uncompromising. "…The natural environment of Hawai'i is one of our planet's most magnificent treasures. The islands are home to more unique species than any place of similar size on earth…But our current efforts are not enough to stem the tide of extinction and time is running out."

In an address to the legislature Governor John Waihe'e recommended quick action on eight of the report's ten proposals. These included a request for permanent funding for one of the most innovative environmental protection programs in the nation. Taketa calls the Natural Area Partnership "the only program of its kind."

About half of Hawai'i's rainforest is privately owned. This program is designed to encourage owners to set aside acreage as preserved land. The state provides matching funds—two dollars for one—to share in management cost. Landowners agree to permanently dedicate significant natural lands. Early in 1992 Maui Land & Pineapple Company granted the Conservancy a perpetual conservation easement, creating a preserve of 8,660 acres in the West Maui Mountains. Called Pu'u Kukui, it is the largest private preserve in Hawai'i, protecting critical watershed as well as three kinds of endangered birds and twenty-seven plant species found nowhere else.

Negotiating such agreements requires more than an affection for the scenery. In 1991 the Conservancy's Hawai'i Heritage program completed the first comprehensive statewide database on the status of Hawai'i's rare species and natural communities. This mix of idealism, diplomacy and informed research has given Taketa and his staff a strong

voice that cuts across political lines and property lines and seems to be speaking on behalf of the earth itself.

Listen to the forest, the kūpuna tell us. Still your mind, says Aitken Roshi, listen for the deep connectedness. Down at the southern edge of Hawai'i's southernmost island they say listen to the rocks. The earth is talking to us, they say, telling us things we need to know about the past, the present and the future. There are in fact so many monitors wired to the rift zones in Ka'ū and Puna that scientists come from around the globe to study the results, to listen with their own ears and see with their own eyes the volcanic region that is the most active on the planet these days, as well as the most thoroughly studied.

Hawaiian Volcano Observatory was established in 1912 by the legendary Thomas Jagger. It has been at the forefront of vulcanology ever since. All U.S. vulcanologists have trained here. Computerized and digitalized, it is a world headquarters for developing techniques for monitoring what a volcano does and why.

The U.S. Geological Survey completed the present facility in 1986. From Kīlauea's rim, the observation tower looks out across the broad, skillet-shaped caldera laced with steam plumes. They waver in the stillness like little banners reminding you of what lies underground. Half a mile or so below Kīlauea lives the magma chamber, the great reservoir of molten matter connected to a "hot spot" farther down. As the Pacific plate drifts north and west by an inch or two per year, each island has been formed above this hot spot, with the Big Island still in process, still growing. This is one of the keys to Hawai'i's role in the world of volcano studies.

Another key is the character of the magma. It is hotter, less viscous, more fluid, so that gasses can percolate through it, which means less pressure building underground. You get

earthquakes here, you get fire fountains a thousand feet high, you get orange rivers that make steam cauldrons as they pour into the sea. But you don't get the terrifying devastation that took so many lives in the Philippines in 1990 when Mount Pinatubo exploded. Here scientists can work systematically over long periods and gather data oftentimes available nowhere else.

Inside Kīlauea there is a smaller crater called Halema'uma'u, according to tradition the home of Pele, the volcano goddess. The observatory stands on a bluff directly above this sacred pit—another of those startling contrasts, like the wild peaks joined to Honolulu's skyline. For centuries Halema'uma'u was a seething lava lake. Hawaiians call it "The Navel of the World," a place where the earth is continually born and reborn. The image offers a handy way to think of the work they do at Hawaiian Volcano Observatory. The focus is on the habits and hazards of the Big Island. The larger subject is how the earth shapes and recreates itself. Vulcanologists stand at the cutting edge of destruction and creation. As they monitor the bulges and bendings, as the magma moves, as it bursts forth to extend the shoreline, to build another lake or shield cone, they help us understand how this globe is behaving and how it behaved a million, or fifty million years ago. Gradually we all learn more about how our habitat came to be the way it is, as well as what the future holds.

In this respect the scientists at Kīlauea have quite a bit in common with another team working some 30 miles away, where another profound feature of Hawai'i's landscape has created another extraordinary opportunity for research. Astronomers regard Mauna Kea (snowy mountain) as the planet's most desirable place to stand and gaze toward the heavens. Far from the glare of an urban center, above much of the air

Raised in Hawai'i Robert Aitken first encountered Zen Buddhism while a prisoner of war in Japan. Now, as Aitken Roshi, he leads Hawai'i's Diamond Sangha, which belongs to Sanbo Kyodan, a lay stream of Soto Zen. He is one of a very few Americans to be designated a "roshi," or Zen master, and his book, Taking the Path of Zen, is considered one of the clearest statements on the subject available in English. Inset: A stone statue of Jizo, protector of children, in the garden of the Diamond Sangha in Pālolo Valley, O'ahu.

turbulence that dims and blurs starlight, this peak is the ideal spot for the Keck Observatory, home of the most powerful piece of equipment ever devised for studying the galaxies.

Previously the most efficient large lens—200 inches wide—was found in the Hale Telescope atop Mount Palomar, near San Diego. For years astronomers considered it unrealistic to build anything larger, due to the weight and distortion that would result from sagging glass. In 1980 some University of California scientists, led by Professor of Astronomy and current Project Scientist Jerry Nelson, proposed a revolutionary system. Smaller segments could significantly reduce the unwieldy weight. Thirty-six segments, in a honeycomb pattern, could be continually aligned under computer control to form a light-gathering surface 33 feet wide, twice the size of the Hale Telescope and four times more powerful.

This spring the last segment, a hexagon of glass weighing 880 pounds, was lowered into place. Astronomers can now peer far deeper into the universe. They talk about receiving light that has travelled 186,000 miles per second for nine billion years. Looking that far into space, of course, means looking that far back in time, back to the earliest eras of the universe, when galaxy clusters were just starting to form.

Maybe this visionary search suggests a way to think about the future of Hawai'i, and the necessary connections between the future and the past. What they're doing on Mauna Kea calls to mind what others have been doing at sea level with the double-hulled sailing canoe.

A project of the Honolulu-based Polynesian Voyaging Society, the sixty-foot *Hōkūle'a* was modeled after ocean-crossing vessels of earlier times. In 1976 it sailed from Hawai'i to Tahiti without instruments, making a reality of what many

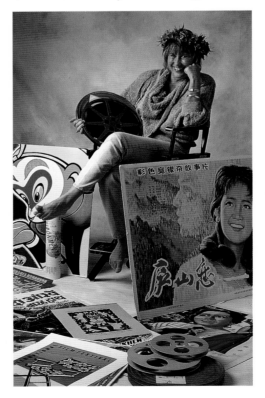

had believed to be mythology, a mid-Pacific fairy-tale. In 1985, guided by navigator Nainoa Thompson, the *Hōkūle'a* set out on a two-year odyssey, from Hawai'i to Tahiti to the Cook Islands, to New Zealand, Tonga and Samoa. The crew covered 12,000 miles by reading wind, stars and currents. These voyages sparked wide interest in navigational feats that preceded by more than a thousand years the period of Europe's global expansion. The claw-sail canoe has become potently symbolic, a double-hulled emblem of ethnic pride for islanders all around the Pacific. With this pride has come new strength. To find it, the Hawaiians had first to sail back many centuries into their own history, to remember almost forgotten skills and reclaim that heritage of seamanship and ocean-going prowess. Now islanders from all over the Pacific turn to Nainoa and the *Hōkūle'a* crew to regain this knowledge.

These voyages, through space and over water, are instructive for us all. They are about the quest that never dies, the quest for knowledge of our origins, the yearning to know or to remember where we came from, how we got to be the way we are. In the *Tao Te Ching* Lao Tzu says, "The way that leads forward seems to lead backward."

With seismometers and print-outs the geologist tracks magma flow to tell us how the ground we stand on got here. With lenses computer-adjusted to the nanometer, the astronomer looks back nine billion years to tell us how our universe began. The wilderness manager and the roshi both remind us to acknowledge and honor our age-old kinship with all the other forms of life. A first-grade teacher wants to keep her ancestral language alive so that words themselves can link a child's future to the wisdom of the past.

—James D. Houston

Every year, 25,000
Oʻahu schoolchildren
take a one-day field
trip into lush Mākiki
Valley to look under
rocks, fish in a stream
and crack open kukui
nuts. Their host in
the valley is the Hawaiʻi
Nature Center, a
non-profit environmen-
tal education orga-
nization which believes
that children will
develop personal, caring
relationships with
the natural world if
they are given the
chance to muck about
it. Bishop Museum's
ʻŌhiʻa Project—unique
in the nation—trained
1,400 teachers to
implement a natural
history curriculum for
grades one through
eight. Following pages:
Dr. Yoshihiko Sinoto
of the Bishop Museum
examines rock art on
Easter Island for future
conservation.

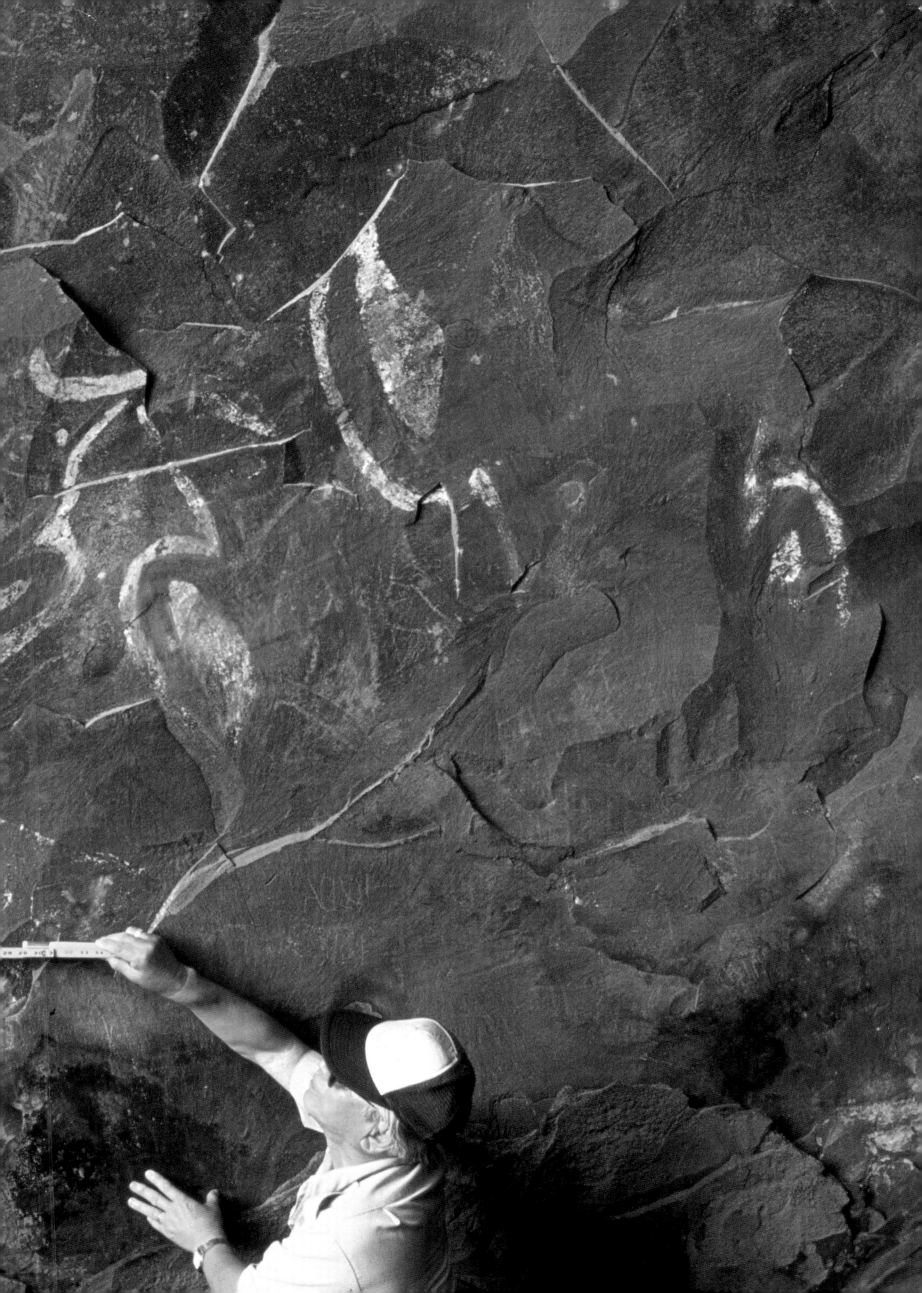

Opposite: Papa Henry Auwae is a kahuna lāʻau lapaʻau, a master of Hawaiian medicine and healing. His pharmacy is the forest. He prays to the spirits of the living plants, asks permission before taking curative roots, stems, leaves, fruit or seeds. His knowledge, passed to him from his great-great-grandmother, will survive through his teaching. This page: At a tidepool near Hāna, Maui, scientists Gary Bignami and Paul Grothaus locate a rare patch of limu-make-o-Hāna, an extremely poisonous soft coral into which Hawaiian warriors once dipped their spears. The palytoxin found in the coral has led to a decade's worth of promising anti-cancer research involving the University of Hawaiʻi and Hawaiʻi Biotechnology Group.

⊾ ⟨⟨⟨⟨ ⊾ ⟨⟨⟨⟨ ⊾⟨⟨⟨⟨
Frank De Lima, Hawai'i's reigning master of ethnic comedy, once trained for the priesthood. Now he performs nightly in Waikīkī and daily at schools, where he combines humor with no-nonsense advice about reading, studying, laughter and family. De Lima's comic ministry involves annual visits to every public elementary and intermediate school in Hawai'i and many private schools. K–3 kids get the "Peanut-Butter-and-Jelly Talk"; 4–6th graders get "Tidah-itis and Blalah-itis: Diseases of Attitude"; and 7–8th graders get "Self-Esteem and General Review."

Throughout the month of April, Chinese families laden with food and drink gather at ancestral graves to welcome returning spirits temporarily released from the netherworld. At Honolulu's Mānoa Chinese Cemetery, they leave pork, fish, tea and whiskey—even lit cigars—on the graves and burn slips of paper printed to look like money so the returning spirits can once again enjoy the pleasures of life. Children play hide-and-seek among the polished stones. The 3,000-year-old Ching Ming festival begins ceremonially on April 5 with firecrackers, roast pigs and music. For a moment, the barrier between then and now loses its opacity.

CHAPTER SIX

BEYOND THE REEF

Out on the lanai at twilight, enjoying the steady breeze and the view down Pālolo Valley to the sea, I reflected for maybe the thousandth time on what a pleasant place Hawai'i is to call home. And I started ticking off a list of reasons: the climate, the beauty of the islands, our genial, tolerant mix of people. I added the ocean close by, fresh air, plate lunches and mangoes in season, even though my tree let me down this year. Most of the things on the list, I noticed, feel good either on the skin or in the belly—it was a pretty superficial list, when you got right down to it. If the breeze hadn't been so cool and the sounds rising up from the valley so soothing, I might have pursued this line of thought to an unsettling conclusion.

"Lucky Come Hawai'i," Maui writer Jon Shirota titled his famous, funny book, and most of us would agree. We love our islands, and in a way quite unlike anywhere else in the world I've ever been, they seem to love us back. Those long green arms reaching down from the Pali almost to Waikīkī may have houses on them now, but they still calm our senses and refresh our spirits. Even in a city the size of Honolulu, you feel that the world of nature, with its vast healing and procreative powers, is sustaining us in our ordinary lives, making us a little healthier, a little livelier, maybe even a little happier on particularly splendid days.

The tradewinds clear away more than the detritus of our power plants and automobiles—they seem to clear some useless ideas from our minds as well. At least people get long here. Every day I hear a half-dozen different languages right around one Honolulu neighborhood: there's Korean at the sundry mart, Japanese at the flower store, Vietnamese at the restaurant, Chinese at the manapua store and even a few words of Okinawan at our local produce shop. You can find this phenomenon in any big city in the United States; what's unique here is the way different ethnic groups fit naturally into our shared local culture. The Hawaiians, with their hugely generous spirit of inclusiveness, created the basis for this equable state of affairs when they accepted wave after wave of newcomers to the Islands. Now the one language you seldom hear around anymore is Hawaiian.

This is the kind of unsettling observation that invades pleasant musings out on the lanai, making me realize that my list of agreeable things about life in Hawai'i just scratches the surface. I suspect that there are profoundly rich and rewarding aspects of life in these Islands that I'm as remote from now as I was fifteen years ago just off the plane.

I wish I knew more about the landforms with their place names, and about the plants and animals around us here. I wish I knew the Hawaiian language, and the view of the world it carries in its structure, syntax and vocabulary. Sometimes I feel like making an offering of gratitude for the air we breathe and the earth we walk on, but I don't know how. Benefitting so tangibly from the privilege of living here, I'm at a loss when it comes to expressing my appreciation in an authentic way.

I once lived on an island where the villagers had a saying about getting to know a place. They said you couldn't settle into their village by liv-

ing there for just ten, twenty or thirty years. It took three generations, and your grandchild would be the first in your family to really be part of the little world of Hoshidate. That may not be true anymore, even on a small Pacific island, but the saying does have the value of passing on the long view: knowledge isn't something you acquire so much as something you settle into.

Now back out on the lanai, everything still as night slips away to the west, I'm counting the good things about Hawai'i again. Our spreading plumeria tree definitely doesn't make the list—it's encroaching on mango territory and needs to be chopped back. My neighbor's rooster, surprisingly, does, now that we get up at the same time. He tells me it's almost dawn now, as with a sigh and a long stretch life in the valley begins to stir.

If it were visible, we'd see the breeze peeking first over the Pali, then easing down above the forest, skirting an outcropping here, dipping into a hollow there, separating into crosscurrents across the valley floor, then finally weakening as the land opens out towards the shore. It's not hard to imagine the breeze being alive, to imagine yourself riding it back up the Pali, down towards Kahalu'u, and then beyond the reef out over the open sea. Blowing around on the breeze, you touch everything—the earth, the ocean, the sky; people even breathe you into their bodies, breathe you out when they sing or yell at each other over some crazy thing.

Thinking about the breeze like this brings me a little closer to the Hawai'i I'm always missing. Maybe the *mana* of the land, carried by the breeze, will someday give the man its gift of wisdom. Most evenings, you'll find me on the lanai, just taking it easy, enjoying the cool breeze down the valley.

—Chris Pearce